THE NEIGHBORHOOD OF BASEBALL

ALSO BY BARRY GIFFORD

Beautiful Phantoms (1981)

Landscape with Traveler (1980)

Port Tropique (1980)

Jack's Book (with Lawrence Lee) (1978)

THE
NEIGHBORHOOD
OF
BASEBALL

A PERSONAL HISTORY OF THE CHICAGO CUBS

BARRY GIFFORD

WRIGLEY FIELD
HOME OF
CHICAGO CUBS
GAMES START ONE THIRTY
NATIONAL LEAGUE CHAMPIONS

E. P. DUTTON   NEW YORK

Published in the United States by Elsevier-Dutton Publishing Co., Inc.,
2 Park Avenue, New York, N.Y. 10016.

Library of Congress Cataloging in Publication Data
Gifford, Barry
The neighborhood of baseball.
1. Chicago. Baseball Club (National League)—History.   I. Title.
GV875.C6G53   796.357'64'0977311   80-28597
ISBN 0-525-16457-X

Published simultaneously in Canada by
Clarke, Irwin & Company, Limited, Toronto and Vancouver

Designed by Mary Beth Bosco

First Edition

10 9 8 7 6 5 4 3 2 1

This book is for my children, Asa Colby Gifford
and Phoebe Lou Gifford, and for
my old companion at the ball park, Steve Friedman.

And for the WBA.

ACKNOWLEDGMENTS
For their help, spirit, expertise and—most of all—
friendship, my thanks to Victor "The Chief" Holchak,
"Bat Boy" Jerry Rosen, Tom "Bull" Farber,
"Governor" Ray Mungo, Jim "The Jet" Carothers,
"East Coast Barry" Weiner, "Doctor John" Maesaka,
"Magic Frank" Malitz, Barry Copilow, Davey Rogoff,
Penn "The Mad Dane" Jensen, and Donald Waful.
And to Ray Neinstein in right field.

Thanks also, for their various assistance, to
Joyce Malitz, Paul Ostrof, Beverly Carothers,
Mike Carothers, Stu Smith, Buck Peden, Paul De Angelis,
Don Ellis, Mary Louise Nelson and Elizabeth Nelson,
and Dorothy Marjorie Colby.

"Barry Gifford, ex–University of Missouri star, hitting over .500 in obscurity in San Francisco; he could be Bobby Murcer but Bobby Murcer could not be him."*

—RICHARD GROSSINGER, from "Baseball Voodoo" in the anthology *Baseball Diamonds* (Garden City, N.Y.: Doubleday/Anchor, 1980)

"The greatest spot in the world is Wrigley Field in Chicago because there you have afternoon baseball. The game was made to be played in the daytime."

—SHAG CRAWFORD, National League umpire 1956–75

---

*Bobby Murcer, an outfielder, has played for the New York Yankees, San Francisco Giants, and Chicago Cubs.

CONTENTS

ILLUSTRATIONS

AUTHOR'S NOTE

This book is a personal history. It is, therefore, a highly subjective portrait of a time, basically the early 1950s through the mid-'60s; a place, Chicago (specifically my old neighborhood, with an interlude or two elsewhere in the Midwest); and a team, the Chicago Cubs of those years. It has not been my intent to provide a comprehensive examination of any of the above. The neighborhood of the title exists now and forever in my memory, and because of that I am its sole chronicler. What I offer the reader is a brief tour around the block and down the street. If some of the things encountered seem a bit unbelievable, then I beg the reader's indulgence and politely suggest he suspend his doubts for the rest of the way, if only to more suitably appreciate the landscape and what it may include. That the Chicago Cub baseball teams discussed here were something less than the world-beaters I wished them to be there can be no doubt. But they were there when I was, and perhaps the most important fact to be recognized is that we both survived and they sufficed.

—B.G.

PART 1
THE PAST RECAPTURED

And—while you live and I—shall last
Its tale of seasons with us yet
Who cherish, in the undying past,
The men we never can forget.

—MARCEL PROUST

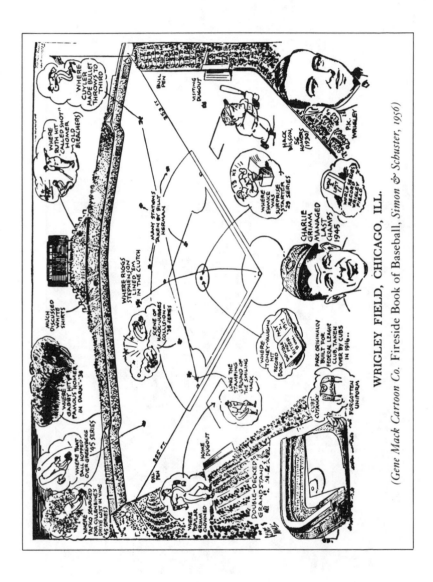

WRIGLEY FIELD, CHICAGO, ILL.

(Gene Mack Cartoon Co. Fireside Book of Baseball, *Simon & Schuster, 1956*)

ONE

I was born in 1946, one year after the Chicago Cubs last won the National League pennant. As of this writing that was thirty-five years ago, and the prospects of the club's reversing that trend in the foreseeable future are bleak. So bleak, in fact, and so obviously apparent to even the most diehard Chicago Cub fans, that on opening day of the 1980 season a group of fans in the bleachers in Wrigley Field, the Cubs' home playing grounds since 1916 (when it was known legitimately as Cubs Park), unfurled a banner—on opening day, mind you—that read: WAIT TILL NEXT YEAR!

During the decade and some from the mid-1950s through the mid-'60s that I regularly attended approximately fifty Cub games a year, I had little company. Baseball had not, on the North Side of Chicago, anyway, become quite the entertainment spectacle it is expected to be today, and crowds regularly numbered in the hundreds—especially when the opponents were such equally ill gathered aggregations as the Philadelphia Phillies of the '50s or the New York Mets of the early '60s. Between 1952, when I began to attend games regularly, and 1964, when I left Chicago, the Cubs finished as high as fifth—out of eight teams (after 1962, ten) —only three times, tying another club for that small distinction each time. During that period they finished dead last twice, seventh (out of eight) five times, eighth (out of ten) once. In 1962 they managed to finish ninth, ahead only of the fledgling and widely ridiculed Mets; in 1966 they wound up tenth, the Mets having surpassed them. To add further ignominy, the Mets beat the

3

Cubs out of the pennant in 1969, and won again in 1973 while the Cubs continued on their mediocre path.

Why? And why again. Why have the Cubs done so miserably over the years? And second, why, since the mid-'60s, have they so consistently drawn such good crowds? Why also are so many loyal Cub fans spread near and far? Fans that live and die (mostly the latter) with each season's early rise and predictable fall, a trend begun during Leo Durocher's reign (1966–mid-'72). Is it because the Cubs are the last team to play all of their home games during the day? (Wrigley Field, as a concession to neighborhood residents, has never installed lights for night games.) Is it because Wrigley Field, with its ivy-covered outfield wall, is perhaps the most beautiful of all major league ball parks? Is it because the Cubs have so firmly established themselves since the end of World War II, the *new* modern era, as the most legitimate—certainly the most consistent—of underdogs, thereby gaining identification by the average fan?

I don't believe there is any one answer. I do believe baseball was made to be played in daylight, just as I am of the not un-prejudiced (as a native Chicagoan—a *North*sider—some words regarding the South Side anon) persuasion that Wrigley Field is indeed the most splendid of stadia designed for the express pur-pose of housing games of modified rounders, only Fenway Park in Boston and The House That Ruth Built coming close. I can also swallow that fans identify and sympathize with the under-dog, but at bottom none of these things is the whole story. I suppose I don't really care why the Cubs have such a plethora of devotees, I know only that I am one and that I find it impossible —inconceivable—to give my heart to another, however talented or untalented, bunch of ballplayers performing in whatever city in this country or any other. (I am happy for those Canadians who appreciate baseball, but it's still difficult for me to accept the fact that two major league franchises reside north of the United States border—I mean, I can't *really* accept even Los Angeles and San Francisco, let alone Anaheim, Seattle, San Diego, Houston, or Arlington, Texas—Arlington, Texas!—as valid major league venues. Some are not.) But that's my problem, born of having come of age in the Midwest when there were only eight teams in each major league and every one of them was east of the Mississippi River.

So that's what this book is really about, being a boy in the largest city in Illinois just after World War II and losing my heart in as unrequited a relationship anyone ever could have with a ball team. I say "have" because it's an ongoing thing, this unrequited business. I'm thirty-three years old and the Cubs still haven't won. Stranger still, though for fully half of those years I have not lived in Chicago, I remain a Cub fan. I am forever asking Giant and A's fans if they've heard the score of the Cubs' game and getting strange looks for it. I suppose to some it might appear a sad history, or—to those uninterested in the doings of professional baseball—a peculiar aberration on my part. I'm assured there are as equally rabid, dedicated—and disappointed—Red Sox, Phillies, and Tiger fans. I've even met a few. But it's difficult for me to imagine anyone being *really* concerned about any team but the Cubs. How did it happen?

---

*This was written prior to Philadelphia's victory in the 1980 World Series.

TWO

My grandfather never wore an overcoat. That was Ezra, my father's father, who had a candy stand under the Addison Street elevated tracks near Wrigley Field. Even in winter, when it was ten below and the wind cut through the station, Ezra never wore more than a heavy sport coat, and sometimes, when Aunt Belle, his second wife, insisted, a woolen scarf wrapped up around his chin. He was six feet two and two hundred pounds, had his upper lip covered by a bushy mustache, and a full head of dark hair until he died at ninety, not missing a day at his stand till six months before.

He never told anyone his business. He ran numbers from the stand and owned an apartment building on the South Side. He outlived three wives and one of his sons, my father. His older son, my Uncle Bruno, looked just like him, but Bruno was mean and defensive whereas Ezra was brusque but kind. He always gave me and my friends gum or candy on our way to and from the ball park, and he liked me to hang around there or at another stand he had for a while at Belmont Avenue, especially on Saturdays so he could show me off to his regular cronies. He'd stand me on a box behind the stand and keep one big hand on my shoulder. "This is my *grandson,*" he'd say, and wait until he was sure they had looked at me—I was the first and then his only grandson, Uncle Bruno had two girls—"Good *boy!*"

He left it to his sons to make the big money, and they did all right, my dad with the rackets and the drugstore, Uncle Bruno as an auctioneer, but they never had to take care of the old man, he took care of himself.

Ezra spoke broken English; he came to America with his sons (my dad was seven, Bruno fourteen) and a daughter from Vienna in 1918. I always remember him standing under the tracks outside the station in February, cigar stub poked out between mustache and muffler, waiting for me and my dad to pick him up. When we'd pull up along the curb my dad would honk but the old man wouldn't notice. I would always have to run out and get him. I figured Ezra always saw us but waited for me to come for him. It made him feel better if I got out and grabbed his hand and led him to the car.

"Pa, for Chrissakes, why don't you wear an overcoat?" my dad would ask. "It's cold."

The old man wouldn't look over or answer right away. He'd sit with me on his lap as my father pointed the car into the dark.

"What cold?" he'd say after we'd gone a block or two. "In the *old* country was cold."

THREE

I like to think of my father's father and his pals as typical of the old-guard sports fans of my early boyhood. It was from my grandfather Ezra's lips that I first heard the name "Cavarretta," and Ezra really couldn't have cared less about the Cubs. He was a horse player, an affliction that would envelop me in my mid-to-late teens. But it was Ezra whom I distinctly recall vilifying the Cub manager of '52 for his strategical ineptitude regarding some maneuver or other that resulted in the Cubs' finishing in the second division that year.

Philip Joseph Cavarretta, born July 19, 1916, in Chicago, was a marvelous hitter. A slender left-hander, in twenty-two years' service as a first baseman, all in Chicago and all but a year and a trifle with the Cubs, Phil Cavarretta compiled a lifetime batting average of .293. In 1945 he had led the league with .355, and five times averaged better than .300. His was a legendary presence.

Actually, my grandfather had little to complain about regarding the Cubs' placing fifth in 1952. He should have been overjoyed, seeing as how the Cubs had finished last the previous year with Frankie Frisch at the helm for the first 100 games, at which point Cavarretta was made a playing manager, a difficult assignment. In '51 the soon-aspirant television actor Chuck Connors ("The Rifleman") held down the first-base job for most of the season, batting .239. That same season, at the age of thirty-five, Cavarretta, in 206 at bats (Connors had 201 official plate appearances), hit .311. By 1952 Connors was gone to Hollywood, Dee

Fondy became the regular Cub first-sacker (he batted .300 over the full season), and Cavarretta, as pilot, guided the Northsiders to a .500 finish. Not bad in any year. But not really very good, either. I saw my first major league game at Wrigley Field in 1952, sitting in a seat behind the Cub dugout next to my dad in the box bought for the season by the Schenley liquor company—my dad sold liquor in his drugstore on the corner of Chicago and Rush. The Cubs won, I remember that, they looked good. But the next year, with Cavarretta still at the helm, they finished in seventh place, 24 games below .500.

It was a proper beginning for a young fan. Maybe Connors saw it coming and that's why he went West. As for me, I had no choice, I was hooked. At five years old I could hardly go anywhere on my own, and I'd been exposed to the Chicago Cubs. I see it now as being a bit like the lure and dilemma of the South Seas for Gauguin, all that overwhelming beauty with nary an early sign of the insidious secret to be one day suddenly revealed in all its irrevocable and horrible truth.

FOUR

Phil Cavarretta, the National League's most valuable player of 1945, was the first great Cub name that I remember. Old-timers mentioned Hack Wilson, who hit the National League record 56 homers in 1930, driving in 190 runs to boot, also a record—even now—but Wilson played in the '20s and '30s, ancient history. Even Cavarretta's day was past. The new Cub hero was Hank Sauer, the power-hitting outfielder who in 1952 led the National League in home runs with 37 and runs batted in with 121.

Sauer, whom I would later see often in uniform as batting coach with the San Francisco Giants, was the dominant batsman on those early-50s Cub teams. The thing I remember most about Sauer is how sad-faced he seemed, how, despite his tough appearance, almost wistful he looked, as if he wanted to be someplace else.

Outfielder Frankie Baumholtz, who came to the Cubs from Cincinnati in 1949, batted better than .300 in '52 and '53 and hit .297 in '54, was a solid player, a clutch performer who in 1955 and 1956 (the latter with the Phillies) led the National League in pinch hits. Baumholtz had also played pro basketball for two years, and had been a decent scorer, averaging 10.5 points a game for Youngstown in the 1945–46 season and 14 points a game for Cleveland in 1946–47. Baumholtz was a good athlete, but other than he and Sauer, Cavarretta being past his prime, that 1952 Cub team had no really potent sticks.

A case could be made, I suppose, for the new first baseman,

Phil Cavarretta (Wide World)

Dee Fondy, who hit .300 three times in his eight major league seasons, and in '53 had his finest year, batting .309, with 18 home runs and 78 RBI, but his was a limited talent. After '53 he tailed off considerably, and he never was one to really capture the fans' imagination.

Pitchers Bob Rush and Warren Hacker had okay seasons in '52, winning 17 and 15 games respectively, each with earned run averages below 3, but they collapsed in '53—Hacker led the league in losses with 19. Righthander Johnny Klippstein became a predictable performer in 1953, seeming always to be throwing a gopher ball in the bottom of the ninth. He and Turk Lown were the Cubs' main relief pitchers, appearing in 48 and 49 games respectively, and compiling equally egregious ERA's of 4.83 and 5.16.

The 1953 infield of Fondy, second baseman Eddie Miksis, shortstop Roy Smalley, and third baseman Randy Jackson made a total of 88 errors, Fondy and Miksis leading the league for that dubious distinction at their positions. Even Sauer slumped in '53, hitting only 19 home runs and driving in just 60. The bright spot —other than Fondy's .309 average—was the early-season acquisition from Pittsburgh of slugger Ralph Kiner, who belted 28 homers for the Cubs, 35 in all that year. But Kiner was a terrible outfielder and was at the end of his road; in two years he would be retired from the game.

The early and mid-'50s were the years of Brooklyn's "boys of summer," Campanella, Robinson, Furillo, et al. Nobody cared about the Cubs but Cub fans, who were far fewer then than now. The best thing that can be said in retrospect about that 1953 Cub team is that it was only one year away from the era of Ernie Banks. Banks, who would clearly establish himself as one of the great hitters in the majors by 1955, got into 10 games at the end of the '53 season, batting .314 and hitting 2 homers. For eight more years at shortstop and ten at first base Banks, a youthful veteran of the Negro Leagues, where he played for the Kansas City Monarchs, would, despite the oft heard complaint that he couldn't hit in the clutch (though as Willie Mays noted about a similar complaint directed at another player, Ted Williams, you don't drive in 1,636 runs, as Banks did, without coming through in the clutch *once* in a while!), delighted not only Cub fans but fans in every city in which his team played. If not quite the Cubs' salvation, Ernie became the fans' balm, belting 512 home runs during his lifetime.

I have an indelible image in my mind of the young Ernie Banks at the plate, nervously moving his fingers as he gripped the thin bat handle, fingering it as if it were a vertically held piccolo, arms back, cocked by those long, slender wrists, head slightly forward on his slim—to the end of his career—body. The snap of those magical wrists was electric, like Hank Aaron's in his Milwaukee Brave years and later Billy Williams's. For such an unassuming-appearing man as Banks to generate such awesome power was never easy to reconcile. So calm, so slim, so sudden, and the ball so swift in its arrowlike arc toward Waveland Avenue. "Bingo" we used to call Banks in the '50s. "It's a great day for a ball game," Ernie would announce each afternoon, smiling that beautiful smile of his, "let's play two." The man had an indomitable spirit, which was most fortunate for him, because in nineteen big league seasons with the Cubs, despite winning two most valuable player awards, three home run titles, and two RBI crowns, appearing in numerous All-Star games, setting a record for fewest errors in a season by a shortstop (since broken), becoming the only shortstop in major league history to accumulate 80 extra-base hits in a season (he did it three times, with a high of 83 in 1957) until Robin Yount of the Milwaukee Brewers accomplished the feat in 1980, he never once played in a World Series.

FIVE

Pops, my other grandfather, my mother's father, and his brothers spent much of their time playing bridge and talking baseball in the back room of their fur coat business. From the time I was four or five Pops would set me up on a high stool at a counter under a window looking down on State Street and give me a furrier's knife with a few small pelts to cut up. I spent whole afternoons that way, wearing a much-too-large-for-me apron with the tie strings wrapped several times around my waist, cutting up mink, beaver, fox, squirrel, even occasional leopard or seal squares, careful not to slice my finger with the razor-sharp mole-shaped tool, while the wet snow slid down the high, filthy State and Lake Building windows and Pops and my Great-Uncles Ike, Nate, and Louie played cards.

They were all great baseball fans, they were gentlemen, and didn't care much for other sports, so even in winter the card-table talk tended to be hot-stove league speculation about off-season trades or whether or not Sauer's legs would hold up for another season. Of course there were times customers came in, well-to-do women with their financier husbands, looking as if they'd stepped out of a Peter Arno *New Yorker* cartoon; or gangsters with their girl friends, heavy-overcoated guys with thick cigars wedged between leather-gloved fingers. I watched the women model the coats and straighten their stocking seams in the four-sided full-length mirrors. I liked dark mink the best, those ankle-length, full-collar, silk-lined ones that smelled so good with left-over traces of perfume. There was no more luxurious feeling than to nap under my mother's own sixty-pelt coat.

By the time the fur business bottomed out, Pops was several years dead—he'd lived to eighty-two—and so was Uncle Ike, at eighty-eight. Pops had seen all of the old-time greats, Tris Speaker, the Babe, even Joe Jackson, who he said was the greatest player of them all. When the White Sox clinched the American League pennant in 1959, the first flag for them in forty years (since the Black Sox scandal of 1919), he and I were watching the game on television. The Sox were playing Cleveland, and after the Sox turned over one of their 141 double plays of that season, Aparicio to Fox to Big Ted Kluszewski to end it, Pops clicked off the set in disgust. "Lousy Cubs," was all he said.

Uncle Nate and Uncle Louie kept on for some time, going in to work each day not as furriers but to Uncle Louie's Chicago Furriers Association office. He'd founded the association in the '20s—in "Charlie Grimm's day," he'd say—acting as representative to the Chamber of Commerce, Better Business Bureau, and other civic organizations. Louie was also a poet. He'd written verse, he told me, in every form imaginable. Most of those he showed me were occasional poems, written to celebrate coronations—the brothers had all been born and raised in London—and inaugurations of American presidents. In the middle right-hand drawer of his desk he kept boxes of Dutch-shoe chocolates, which he would give me whenever I came to visit him.

Uncle Nate, who lived to be 102, came in to Uncle Louie's office clean-shaven and with an impeccable high-starched collar every day until he was a hundred. He once told me he knew he would live that long because of a prophecy by an old man in a wheelchair he'd helped cross a London street when he was seven. The man had put his hand on Nate's head, blessed him, and told him he'd live a century.

Uncle Louie was the last to go, at ninety-four. Having long since moved away, I didn't find out about his death until a year or so later. The fur business, as my grandfather and his brothers had known it, was long gone; even the State and Lake Building was about to be torn down, a fate that had already befallen

Fritzl's, where the brothers had gone each day for lunch. Fritzl's had been the premier restaurant of the Loop in those days, with large leather booths, big white linen napkins, and thick, high-stemmed glasses. Like the old Lindy's in New York, Fritzl's was frequented by show people, entertainers, including ballplayers, and newspaper columnists. Many of the women who had bought coats, or had had coats bought for them, at my grandfather's place ate there. I was always pleased to recognize one of them, drinking a martini or picking at a shrimp salad, the fabulous dark mink draped gracefully nearby.

SIX

During spring training in 1954 Phil Cavarretta was ousted as manager of the Cubs. He then hefted his perennially potent bat down south to Comiskey Park, where he finished his career, playing two years with the White Sox, batting .316 in 1954 and even stealing 4 bases, something he hadn't accomplished in his last three years with the Cubs. The Sox had a good year, winning 94 games and finishing third behind the Yankees, who won 103, and the Cleveland Indians, who won a remarkable 111 games. Fain, Fox, Minoso, Lollar, Trucks and company must have been a welcome relief for Cavarretta, who was used to something better than he'd been having lately with the Cubs.

Up on the North Side 1945 seemed an eon in the deep past as the Cubs, despite installing their star third baseman of the '30s and '40s, Stan Hack, as skipper, finished a dismal seventh in '54, 8 games back of St. Louis with their rookie of the year Wally Moon and Stan Musial, who hit his usual .330.

The best the Cubs could offer in the way of individual performances in 1954 was the resurgent bat of Hank Sauer, who hit 41 big ones and drove in 103 while averaging a solid .288. And it was Ernie Banks's first full season. Even manager Hack, who was as tough a character as they come but whose intellect was a constant subject of discussion amongst the short-beer habitués of taverns all the way out Milwaukee Avenue, could see Ernie had what it took to be a great one. Banks hit .275, with 19 home runs and 79 RBI. Along with newcomer Gene Baker at second base, who also hit .275, including a surprising 13 homers—Baker would

Willie Mays in the 1954 World Series (Wide World)

later become one of the first black managers in the minor leagues, at Batavia, New York, in the Pittsburgh chain—the Cubs suddenly had their first decent combination in the middle of the infield since Lenny Merullo and Don Johnson in 1945. Baker, however, had an erratic arm, and committed 25 errors, enough to lead the league at his position and inspire television announcer Jack Brickhouse to describe double-play efforts as "Banks to Baker to Addison Street."

Stan Hack had been a tough out in his day, a .301 lifetime hitter (sixteen years in the bigs), and it wasn't easy for him to watch the Cubs flounder. Kiner, Sauer, and Banks kept the fans entertained, however, with the long ball, and Hal Jeffcoat had turned in his outfield glove for a shot as a pitcher, which proved interesting at times as Jeff led the staff in saves despite a 5.19 ERA. Paul Minner and Big Bob Rush hurled the odd decent game, but it was a very mediocre team and 1954, just as '52 and '53 had belonged to Jackie Robinson and company—as would '55 and '56 —belonged to the sensational Giant center fielder Willie Mays, perhaps the greatest baseball player of all time. "The game was made for Willie," Ted Williams said, and there are few who ever saw Mays step on a field who would disagree.

In '54 Willie Mays batted .345, which led the league, cracked 41 home runs, and drove in 110. New York won the pennant over Brooklyn by 5 games, but watching Mays that year I began to realize what the game of baseball could be at its zenith. I was in the Cub Scouts then, and in November our troop was shown films of the World Series played the previous month. The Giants defeated Cleveland 4 games to none, and it was the first game, the game of The Catch, that made it all click for me. Watching Mays put his head down and run and run to catch Vic Wertz's 440-foot fly ball over the shoulder like an end snaring a sixty-five-yard pass for a touchdown was, I'm sure not only for me, a revelation of the truest kind. Willie Mays was built to play ball, he could do everything and made you want to try. Dusty Rhodes hitting those dinky home runs was necessary to the Giants' cause, surely, but it was Willie who made it matter. He was the best I've ever seen.

SEVEN

When I was four and a half years old I was sent to camp in Eagle River, Wisconsin, several hours by train north of Chicago. I was by two and a half years the youngest boy at the camp, which season lasted two months, July and August. The campers slept in cabins arranged according to age. I went to the camp for three years (in 1951, '53, and '54) and was always resident in the youngest side of the youngest cabin, called Frontier Lodge.

The name of the camp was Tecumseh Lodge. A small log house, supposedly used by the Shawnee Indian Tecumseh when he was on a campaign to unite the tribes of the Old Northwest —Sauk and Fox, Winnebago, Menominee—was within the camp boundary. Tecumseh had been a great man, we were told at the camp, even though he was an Indian.

My main activity at Tecumseh was trail riding. Each of the riders was given a horse to take care of. The first year I had a calico named Chico, an easygoing older horse. Since I was so young, and could mount Chico only by standing on a box or being lifted aboard, the riding master, Cy Sullivan, didn't expect too much of me. I was a pretty good horseman for four and a half years old, though, the only really unfortunate incident occurring when once I lagged behind the group and kicked Chico to catch up. I was jolted off by his sudden start and rolled down an incline into a clump of bushes. It frightened me, I was a little banged up and refused to get back on Chico, so Cy Sullivan had to put me up on his horse, Pepper, with him.

The second and third years I had a horse named Moonlight, a wilder black horse with a patch of white on his forehead. I never fell off Moonlight, but he was harder to handle than Chico. Some of the older boys had gentler horses, and I was proud that Cy had such confidence in me.

In fact, one night when the horses broke out of the corral Cy enlisted me in the roundup party. It took until dawn to collect them. It was beautiful to see the horses running loose like that. I was with one of the counselors, Warren Eagle, an Ojibway Indian, who did the roping and bridling. I rode the horse bareback back to the corral. I liked Warren the best of all the counselors, probably because he was a devoted Cub fan whose favorite player was Hank Sauer.*

By my third year at Tecumseh I was old enough—I skipped the year after my first year because the camp owner thought it best that I "mature" some, as he told my parents, before returning—even though I was still the smallest kid in camp (it was easy for me to find my place in line at morning reveille—since we lined up according to height, I was always the first!), to attend the occasional "socials" with the neighboring girls' camp, Jack O'Lantern. These dances were always scheduled on Saturday nights, which was when the Nighthawks, the elite trail-riding group of which I was a member, went on special pathfinding patrols. We were supposed to individually follow a subtly marked trail blazed by Cy Sullivan and were graded according to the time it took to complete the ride. Some of the trails were extremely difficult to follow, and Cy often had to go out after lost riders.

So I would usually swagger late into the dance dressed in my dusty trail jeans and boots, feeling lean and wiry and tough

---

*An irresistible sidenote: According to Chicago musicologist Arnold Passman, who worked as a waiter at Tecumseh Lodge in 1952, the camp chef was Pete Pipp, brother of Wally Pipp, the Chicago-born New York Yankee first baseman of the 'teens and '20s. Wally Pipp earned everlasting trivia question notoriety by being replaced in a game by Lou Gehrig, who began that day his record Iron Man streak of 2,130 consecutive games.

---

compared to the other boys who'd put on Banlon shirts and slacks and had their hair combed neat. Even though I wasn't quite eight years old I could play the role, lean against a post chewing gum and casually look over the girls on the dance floor. The boys who'd been on the trail ride tried to appear as aloof as possible. After all, we were the Nighthawks, cowboys, and wanted to make sure everyone knew we were special.

I was afraid of the girls, though. All during the time on the trail I couldn't help but think about the dance later, and what I could say to the girls. Most of the time I didn't dance, just stood around and watched, drank bug juice, and tried not to look anybody in the eye.

But once in a while I'd spot a girl I really liked the looks of and ask her to dance. The few times I did this the girls turned out to be a year or so older than me. I told them some ridiculous stories, about how I'd been raised in the desert in Mexico by bandits and used to kill snakes with my pocket knife, then skin and eat them, crazy stories. I didn't really care whether or not they believed me, I just liked to tell the stories. I never knew what I was going to say, and even then the nicest audience I could imagine was a pretty girl who didn't quite know what to make of me.

Life in Frontier Lodge wasn't so good. Most of the counselors were insensitive to the kids, didn't care about them. When it came time to pack the campers' trunks at the end of the summer they'd throw anybody's stuff anywhere. I always wound up back home with three pairs of gym shoes that weren't mine, no underwear, one pair of pants, thirty T-shirts, and everyone else's socks.

One year my dad sent me up a case of my favorite Whiz and Tango candy bars, which I put under my, or really my bunkmate's, bunk, since I slept on top. My bunkmate was a bed wetter, though, and the first night he peed right through the mattress and the thin cardboard cover of the box of candy bars and ruined them.

Bed wetters had a tough time. Every morning you could see them, like lepers in India, dragging their sheets and mattresses out the back doors of the lodges to dry in the sun while the counselors kept their distance and told them to hurry up.

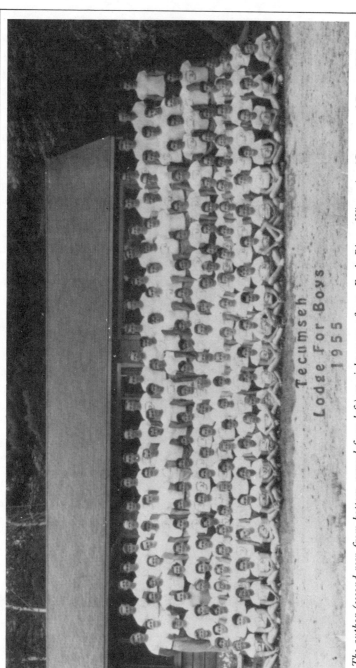

The author (second row from bottom, second from left) at eight years of age. Eagle River, Wisconsin. (Courtesy of Barry Gifford)

The single great event of the summer was the Green and White War. Those were the camp colors. Half of the boys wore green T-shirts with the head of an Indian in a war bonnet outlined in white, and the other half wore white T-shirts with the head of an Indian in a war bonnet outlined in green, both emblazoned with the words TECUMSEH LODGE across the top.

The war was a series of track and field events. I always ran the short sprints, forty, fifty, and sixty yards, and one leg of the final event, the cross-country race. My third and last year at Tecumseh I came in second in all three sprints to a kid from Milwaukee named Barney Kaminski. In previous years I had always won at least one or two of those races, but Kaminski was too fast for me—he was older by about six months, and much bigger—even so he only beat me by a couple of steps each time. Going into the last race, the White team was ahead of the Green by a small margin. My team could still win the war if we beat the White in the cross-country.

I was scheduled to run the next to last lap, but one of my team, the kid who was supposed to run the first lap, wasn't feeling well and couldn't run. Warren Eagle, who was our coach that year, told me to run the first lap instead, but I wanted to run the penultimate lap: it was the longest and most important part of the race, and Kaminski was going to run the final leg for the Whites. I wanted to make sure my team had a big enough lead so that Kaminski couldn't possibly pull it out.

Warren said that I could run both laps but it meant that after I'd completed the first lap I'd have to run a half mile across the grounds to be in position for the other lap. Warren was afraid I would be too tired, but I told him I could do it, there'd be enough time to rest if I just kept on running after the first stretch. I could sit on the hill above the camp for a half hour while I waited for the runner to get there.

I won the first lap, but only by a little, and immediately after handing off the baton I cut across to the hill on the edge of the grounds. It was a brutally hot late August afternoon, and by the time I got there I was exhausted. I lay down on the hill panting and sweating. The White team runner was loosening up, stretching and touching his toes. The thirty minutes went by much too quickly. When I saw the White team runner line up in position I jumped up and took a look: the Green and White mid-stretch men were dead even. I took my place, and the White runner and I took the batons together.

Halfway down the hill the White runner had a step on me but then he fell. He got right up again but I was several yards ahead. My side hurt but I didn't want to lose the lead, it was just what our team needed to beat Kaminski. By the time we reached the tennis courts, in full view of the other campers, who were yelling and screaming, the White runner had made up more than half of the difference between us.

Poised on the far side of the courts was Kaminski, wearing a white headband around his curly blond hair, leaning away, right hand held back to take the white baton.

I wasn't going to have enough of a lead to beat him. I handed off my baton three steps ahead of the White team and kept running—I wanted to see what happened. Kaminski was catching up but our anchor man hung on until the last ten yards, where Kaminski passed him and won the race.

The White team mobbed Kaminski. I sat down on the steps of the recreation hall and tried to catch my breath. Warren Eagle came over and sat next to me. He didn't say anything. He really looked like an Indian: his skin was dark, his hair was black, his nose sloped. He always wore a plain white T-shirt, khaki pants with a red and blue beaded belt that said EAGLE RIVER on it, and white socks with unpolished ROTC shoes. We sat there and watched the White team jump around and slap each other on the back.

"You disappointed?" he asked.

I shrugged my shoulders. I was breathing evenly again.

"You coming back next year?"

"I don't know," I said. "Are you?"

"I'm going into the Army. I'll probably be in Korea.

"The Cubs beat Brooklyn yesterday," said Warren.

"Who pitched?"

"Rush."

"Think he'll win twenty?"

"No, but he would if he were with Brooklyn."

The dinner-warning gong rang.

"Watermelon for dessert tonight."

"I don't like watermelon," I said. "I used to, but it makes me nauseated."

We stood up and Warren shook my hand.

"You did all right," he said. "Good luck to you."

"Thanks," I said, and ran off to wash up.

EIGHT

If it hadn't been for Willie Mays, who clouted 51, and Ted Klus-zewski, who bashed 47 for Cincinnati, Ernie Banks would have had his first home run crown in 1955. Banks blasted 44, drove in 117 runs, and averaged .295 in his first big season. Gene Baker was all over the place at second, leading the league in both putouts and assists as well as errors. Fifty-five was Hank Sauer's last season with the Cubs, and it was a toughie. Sauer could manage only a meager .211 average, with 12 homers. Chicago peddled him to the Cardinals for the next season, in which he fared no better, but he experienced a reprise of his talents in 1957 with the Giants when, at the age of thirty-eight, he hit 26 home runs and drove in 79.

But 1955 saw the Dodgers win in a walk and, behind south-paw Johnny Podres, who won two games including a seventh-game shutout, defeat the Yankees in a World Series for the first time. The Cub outfield, which included at various times Sauer, Jim King, Eddie Miksis, Bob Speake, Jim Bolger, and a part-time Frankie Baumholtz, could hardly match up to Brooklyn's Snider, Furillo, and Amoros. The Dodger outfield, compared to the Cub assemblage, seemed to me like a gathering of supermen. I must have seen the film of Sandy Amoros making that amazing, seem-ingly impossible catch of Yogi Berra's fly ball down the left-field line in the sixth inning of the seventh game of the Series a hun-dred times on television sports shows over that winter, and for years afterward on Marty Glickman's show "Speaking of

Sandy Amoros making the catch off Yogi Berra in the 1955 World Series. (UPI)

Sports." I saw an interview with Amoros after the Series, and when asked about the catch, all he could say, in his broken Cuban-English, was, "I jus' ran, that's all, I kep' run, it was all I could do, an' when I reach out . . . the ball"—and at this point Amoros, extending his right, his glove, hand, grinned so that all thirty-two of his teeth were visible—"the ball . . . it was . . . right . . . there."

For the Brooklyn Dodgers it was a good year, and the next was to be almost as good. I remember coming home from school for lunch one afternoon that October and finding Raymond Day, my mother's "heavy housework" man—he cleaned the windows —watching the World Series on television. I sat down with him and watched Robinson steal a base. "That Jackie," Raymond said, "he's the best there is. And so is the Dodgers." For the Chicago Cubs it was a different story altogether.

NINE

The best thing I can remember about baseball on the North Side of Chicago in 1956 was that I came in second for the home run championship of my Little League with nine. The kid who beat me out hit ten. His name was Tommy Hayden, and as irony would have it he was on the mound when I came up to bat for what promised to be, and was, my last time for the season. Hayden was a fine player even then, at nine or ten years old—he turned out to be a star pitcher in high school—and a gutsy one. He could have walked me but instead chose to pitch me fair and square, throwing me a fast ball right down the middle which I cranked like a shot right back at him. He threw up his glove to protect his face and caught the ball. I've always respected Hayden for pitching to me in that situation.

To me, the Cubs were far less exciting. They finished dead last behind Pittsburgh. The snake-bit Hack was breathing his last as a Cub manager—he tried it again for 10 games with the Cardinals in 1958 and fared no better, losing 7 of them—and Ernie Banks was probably wondering if it hadn't been an ill-advised move to have left the Kansas City Monarchs. Ernie had a good year—.297, 28 homers, 85 RBI—considering there weren't many Cub base runners for him to drive home. Walt Moryn and Don Hoak came over from Brooklyn in a deal for Randy Jackson, and Moryn ("Moose") did all right (.285, 23 home runs) but Hoak hadn't yet learned to hit—he was later to star with Cincinnati and Pittsburgh—so they didn't make much of a difference.

The outfield personnel, in addition to Moryn and Monte Irvin, who was sent to Chicago for his last whiff of major league air after a distinguished career with the Giants (and a belated one, also, Irvin having spent a large portion of his prime playing years toiling in the Negro Leagues), included Pete Whisenant (.239), Jim King (who hit 15 homers, almost all of them late in games that were already long lost), and Solly Drake, a switch-hitter who couldn't hit from either side of the plate. Solly had a brother, Sammy, who came up to the Cubs for a cup of coffee in 1960 and again in '61 only to prove that the affliction ran in the family.

The catching, as handled by Harry Chiti and Hobie Landrith, while adequate, did nothing for the team batting average; Chiti hit .212, Landrith .221. Bob Rush and Sad Sam (also known as "Toothpick Sam") Jones, who'd come over the previous season from Cleveland, provided an occasional well-pitched game—Sad Sam had even thrown a no-hitter against Pittsburgh in '55—but again, there was little solace for the Cub fan, and it showed at the gate. In fact, not even the owner, P. K. Wrigley, came. He stayed up in Lake Geneva, Wisconsin, watching the games on TV. Wrigley's absenteeism was a continuous source of humor for Cub fans. "Not even Wrigley can stand to watch," I heard people say on more than one occasion. His greatest, and most remarked upon, absence occurred in 1962 when he failed to attend the major league All-Star game, which was held that year at Wrigley Field.*

The outstanding event of the 1956 regular season, as I remember it, was Pirate first baseman Dale Long hitting 8 home runs in 8 consecutive games, a record. Long would later become a Cub, a familiar pattern of events. As my friend Big Steve would say, *"Everybody* ends up with the Cubs." Frank Robinson broke in with the Reds in '56 and hit 38 homers, a record for a rookie. It was also Jackie Robinson's last season; because of him the National League was rich with black players. The American League

---

*Leo Durocher, in his autobiography *Nice Guys Finish Last*, claims that P. K. Wrigley attended many Cub games, often sitting in unoccupied areas (there were many) of the upper deck, preferring to avoid recognition by the fans. If so, I can certainly understand why.

---

began to suffer because of its reluctance to sign blacks, the Yankees and Boston being the last teams to do so.

Among the top five batting leaders for average, home runs, runs batted in, hits, slugging average, total bases, stolen bases, and runs scored in the National League in 1956 were sixteen black players; in the American League, for the same categories, there were three. Because of its "progressive" policy—it was only forty-seven years into the modern era (post-1900) before a black man wore a major league uniform—the National League turned the tables on the American and became the stronger circuit, a domination that exists to this day. Between 1950 and 1980 the two leagues engaged in 34 All-Star contests; the National League won 28 of them.

But the biggest thrill of the '56 season was Yankee pitcher Don Larsen's perfect game against Brooklyn in the fifth game of the World Series, the first no-hitter in Series history. I watched the game at home on television and I don't remember much about it now except for catcher Yogi Berra leaping up into the six-foot-four Larsen's arms and hanging on in ecstasy after pinch-hitter Dale Mitchell took the last pitch for strike three. I yelled to my mother, who was in the kitchen, "Larsen just pitched a no-hitter!" "Larsen who?" she yelled back. Larsen, of course, would eventually become a Cub.

TEN

One night when I was eleven I was playing baseball in the alley behind my house. I was batting left-handed when I hit a tremendous home run that rolled all the way to the end of the alley and would have gone into the street but an old man turning the corner picked it up. The old man came walking up the alley toward me and my friends, flipping the baseball up in the air and catching it. When he got to where we stood, the old man asked us who'd hit that ball.

"I did," I said.

"It was sure a wallop," said the old man, and he stood there, grinning. "I used to play ball," he said, and my friends and I looked at each other. "With the Cardinals, and the Cubs."

My friends and I looked at the ground or down the alley where the cars went by on Rosemont Avenue.

"You don't believe me," said the old man. "Well, look here." And he held out a gold ring in the palm of his hand. "Go on, look at it," he said. I took it. "Read it," said the old man.

"World Series, 1931," I said.

"I was with the Cardinals then," the old guy said, smiling now. "Was a pitcher. These days I'm just an old bird dog, a scout."

I looked up at the old man. "What's your name?" I asked.

"Tony Kaufmann," he said. I gave him his ring back. "You just keep hitting 'em like that, young fella, and you'll be a big leaguer." The old man tossed my friend Billy the ball. "So long," he said, and walked on up to the end of the alley, where he went in the back door of Beebs and Glen's Tavern.

"Think he was tellin' the truth or is he a nut?" one of the kids asked me.

"I don't know," I said, "let's go ask my grandfather. He'd remember him if he really played."

Billy and I ran into my house and found Pops watching TV in his room.

"Do you remember a guy named Tony Kaufmann?" I asked him. "An old guy in the alley just told us he pitched in the World Series."

"He showed us his ring," said Billy.

My grandfather raised his eyebrows. "Tony Kaufmann? In the alley? I remember him. Sure, he used to pitch for the Cubs."

Billy and I looked at each other.

"Where's he now?" asked my grandfather.

"We saw him go into Beebs and Glen's," said Billy.

"Well," said Pops, getting out of his chair, "let's go see what the old-timer has to say."

"You mean you'll take us in the tavern with you?" I asked.

"Come on," said Pops, not even bothering to put on his hat, "never knew a pitcher who could hold his liquor."

Kaufmann appeared pleased to see us, had a beer with my grandfather, and gave me and Billy each a pat on the head, promising to keep an eye on us as future prospects.

ELEVEN

I must confess that up until 1956 I did harbor a degree of affection for the White Sox. They were Mayor Daley's team, on the South Side, in Bridgeport, far from my neighborhood, but I liked their shortstop, Chico Carrasquel, and Jim Rivera, the wild-man outfielder who was always banging into fences, sliding head first into bases, and falling down at every opportunity. I was a little kid, and that kind of abandoned, overzealous play impressed me.

(A bit of irony I should mention here: from 1876 to 1893, the Chicago entry in the National League was named the White Stockings. It was this team—later called the Colts, then the Orphans—that subsequently, beginning in 1899, was finally named the Cubs. The Chicago White Sox were established, with that name, in 1901.)

The Sox also had Minnie Minoso—Saturnino Orestes Arrieta Armas "Minnie" Minoso—a fine left fielder and .300 hitter with 20-home-run-per-year power. I always did like Minnie, he was colorful and played hard—the difference between Minoso and Rivera was real ability—and I was appalled when the Sox traded Minoso to Cleveland after the 1957 season. I thought it was a mistake and it turned out to be very unfortunate for Minnie, who missed playing on the Sox pennant-winner in 1959. The Sox got Minoso back from the Indians the following year, but it was too late for him. Like Ernie Banks, Minoso, who wound up a sixteen-year veteran with a .298 lifetime average, never got to play in a World Series.

Alfonso (Chico) Carrasquel (Courtesy of Sport Magazine*)*

*Minnie Minoso
(UPI)*

The White Sox also had Sandy Consuegra, a little right-handed curve-baller who was a product of famous Senator scout Uncle Joe Cambria's fecund Cuban connection. Consuegra went 16 and 3 for the Sox in 1954 and was terrific for a couple of years. But the thing that divorced me forever from the Sox was when they let Chico Carrasquel go 28 games into the '56 season to make room for Luis Aparicio. Of course it was the right move, since Little Looie turned out to be one of the all-time great shortstops and base stealers in major league history, but I had early developed that strange, somewhat unexplainable and unreasonable affection for Chico. I still have a marvelous full-color photo of him that I cut out of a 1950 issue of *Sport* magazine tacked up on the wall of my studio. I suppose I just liked the sound of his name, the way Bob Elson, the long-time White Sox announcer, said it on the radio: "Chico Carrrra-skellll, shortstop." It had a magic sound.

Alfonso Colon "Chico" Carrasquel played for four years after 1955, bouncing around from Cleveland to Kansas City to Baltimore. When the Sox sent Chico away they lost me forever. Even in 1959, though the Dodgers were tired from a tight pennant race and having been in a play-off with Milwaukee and the Sox crushed them in the first game of the World Series eleven to nothing, I knew the Dodgers would win. And I *hated* the Dodgers after they moved to Los Angeles in '58—I still do—but the White Sox had traded Carrasquel and Minoso and so sealed their doom.

TWELVE

The '57 Cubs tied with the Pirates for last place. It was Bob Scheffing's first year as manager, and he saw some bright spots in the Cub future, most notably the "Gold Dust Twins," rookie pitchers Dick Drott, who won 15 games while losing 11, and Moe Drabowsky, who won 13. Drott, however, would never again have a winning season, winning only 12 games in the next six seasons, finishing out his career with a dismal 2 and 12 record for Houston in 1963; and Drabowsky didn't do another decent thing until he surfaced as a relief pitcher in the American League in the '60s, starring for Baltimore and Kansas City.

One particularly notable event Drabowsky participated in in 1958 was Stan Musial's 3,000th hit, a double, which Moe served up to Stan the Man at Wrigley Field. I was present at that milestone moment and was one of those who joined in giving Musial a standing ovation, an accolade participated in by Cub as well as Cardinal players. The game was stopped so that Stan could be presented with the ball. Musial, who was then almost thirty-eight years old, hit .337 that season, with 17 homers and 62 runs driven in. As if that were not remarkable enough, considering his age, four years later, by which time he was going on forty-two, Musial batted .330, hit 19 home runs, and drove in 82.

For the rest, the '57 Cubbies had little to smile about other than the irrepressible Banks, who hit 43 homers and drove in 102 runs. Dale Long, acquired from Pittsburgh (he and Dee Fondy exchanged uniforms), was the lone .300 hitter at .305. The Cubs did try out new uniforms that season. I still have a Topp's bubble gum picture card of Bobby Morgan, who loitered in the second-base area much of that year—Gene Baker having been unwisely dispatched to Pittsburgh—wearing a blue cap with yellow stripes on it, a white button on top. The new uniform, too, had stripes, I believe, but it didn't last long. Habiliment, however, was not at fault, and no baseball fan envied Scheffing his position.

Most, in fact, began to doubt his sanity when Scheffing experimented with a journeyman infielder named Jack Littrell at shortstop for 47 games, shifting Banks to third, even though Ernie was fielding flawlessly at his regular spot. Littrell's range was no improvement on Banks's, and he batted an anemic .190. Bobby Adams, the veteran Cincinnati infielder, held down third for most of the season, but he was at the end of the line.

The Cubs needed help not only at third but at catcher, second, center field, and, most of all, in the bullpen. The 1957 season marked the brief but effective appearance of a twenty-seven-year-old outfielder named Frank Ernaga, an ingenuous flash in the pan who knocked a home run in his first at bat and in 20 games that season (35 at bats) hit .314. His was an oft mentioned name for a time as a legitimate prospect. However, after an even briefer spate in '58 (8 official trips to the plate, all as a pinch hitter), he disappeared from Cubdom forever.

It was a busy winter for the Cub front office, probably their best move being the deal that sent relief pitcher Jim Brosnan to St. Louis, where in '59 he wrote a book, *The Long Season*, mostly about that Cardinal club and their manager Solly Hemus (with whom Brosnan did not see eye to eye), sparing the Cubs and Bob Scheffing the further ignominy of being the primary target of Brosnan's critically acerbic—and witty—commentary. The Cubs, as usual, needed all the help they could get.

THIRTEEN

It was difficult not to be a Milwaukee Braves fan in 1957—in fact, from 1953, when the Braves moved their franchise from Boston to the Wisconsin city, through the early '60s, they were a top-notch team. Being only ninety miles from Chicago, the Braves stole the attention of many Cub and White Sox fans. Of course Hank Aaron had established himself as a star almost as soon as he broke in in 1954, and even if the New York media weren't fully aware of his rare and often spectacular skills, Chicago fans knew how devastating a hitter he could be.

Aaron was touted early on in his career as a potential .400 hitter—the closest he came was .355 in 1959—and his home runs (it seemed as if he matched his uniform number—44—with them every year) were a bonus. That he became the all-time major league home run hitter with 755 total for his career is less impressive to me, who watched him play dozens of times, than his ability, like that of Willie Mays, to do it all and do it all well. Before Aaron's last few seasons, when he seemed to exist solely for the purpose of extending his home run total, Bad Henry was a genuinely complete player. That he could hit was well known to anyone in Portland or Miami who could decipher a Braves box score, but those of us privileged to watch him admired his grace in the field and on the bases. Accused by the press of not being an especially adept base runner and perhaps lacking in speed, during a nine-year stretch (1961–68) Aaron stole better than 20 bases 6 times, with a high of 31 in 1963. He slammed 44 homers that season, too.

But Aaron was far from being "the franchise," as Banks had become with Chicago. The 1957 Milwaukee lineup boasted some mighty limb and timber: third baseman Eddie Mathews (512 lifetime home runs), first baseman Joe Adcock (336 lifetime round-trippers, 4 in one game), left fielder Wes Covington (.330 batting average in 1958), center fielder Billy Bruton (85 stolen bases from '53 to '55), second baseman Red Schoendienst (.310 batting average in 1957), catcher Del Crandall (151 homers in an eight-year span), and Hammerin' Hank. My enduring image of Aaron is his swing at a ball just as Cub catcher Cal Neeman was about to snap it into his glove. Instead, Aaron one-handed the fast ball on a low line drive over Wrigley's left-field wall. Neeman looked at his glove to make sure the pitcher hadn't thrown two balls, found it empty, stared out toward left, then rechecked the mitt, finally just shaking his head in amazement as Aaron circled the bases.

Ernie hit some long balls but most of them were high, they floated out of sight. In the early years of his career, Aaron hit shots like the one pulled from Neeman's glove. But the absolutely hardest-hit ball I ever saw (rivaled closely by Reggie Jackson's home run in the 1971 All-Star game at Detroit) was one Roberto Clemente smote at Wrigley in the late '50s. Passing above second base, it was a chest-high line drive and didn't stop rising until it banged off the scoreboard above the bleachers in center field, 440 feet away. (Josh Gibson, the "black Babe Ruth," the legendary Negro Leagues star, was supposed to have hit one off the Wrigley Field scoreboard clock, which is 100 feet high.)

But the '56–'59 Brave team momentarily diverted some of my attention from the Cubs. Behind Spahn, Burdette, and Buhl and that power-laden lineup, Milwaukee finished second in '56, won the whole thing plus the Series over the Yankees in '57, the pennant again in '58, and in '59 lost the flag in a two-game play-off with Los Angeles. I bumped my head on a shelf jumping for joy the moment Eddie Mathews gathered up Gil McDougald's ground ball and stepped on third to force the runner for the final out of the '57 Series. Lew Burdette, the spitballer, won 3 of those games with a 0.67 ERA. It was his finest hour as a major league pitcher—the next season he would lose two Series decisions to

New York hurler Bob Turley, including the deciding seventh game—and the Milwaukee fans were the most loyal and happiest in all of baseball. Little did anyone dream that by the middle of the following decade the Braves would have moved again, to Atlanta, of all places.

FOURTEEN

I always spotted The Chinaman right off. He would be at the number two table playing nine ball with The Pole. Through the blue haze of Bebop's Pool Hall I could watch him massé the six into the far corner.

My buddy Magic Frank and I were regulars at Bebop's. Almost every day after school we hitched down Howard to Paulina and walked half a block past the Villa Girgenti and up the two flights of rickety stairs next to Talbot's Bar-B-Q. Bebop had once driven a school bus but had been fired for shooting craps with the kids. After that he bought the pool hall and had somebody hand out flyers at the school announcing the opening.

Bebop always wore a crumpled Cubs cap over his long, greasy hair. With his big beaky nose, heavy-lidded eyes, and slow, half-goofy, half-menacing way of speaking, especially to strangers, he resembled the maniacs portrayed in the movies by Timothy Carey. Bebop wasn't supposed to allow kids in the place, but I was the only one in there who followed the Cubs, and since Bebop was a fanatic Cub fan, he liked to have me around to complain about the team with.

The Chinaman always wore a gray fedora and a sharkskin suit. Frank and I waited by the Coke machine for him to beat The Pole. The Pole always lost at nine ball. He liked to play one-pocket but none of the regulars would play anything but straight pool or nine ball or rotation. Sometimes The Pole would hit on a tourist for a game of eight ball but even then he'd usually lose, so Frank and I knew it wouldn't be long before we could approach The Chinaman.

When The Chinaman finished off The Pole he racked his cue, stuck The Pole's fin in his pocket, lit a cigarette, and walked to the head. Frank followed him in and put a dollar bill on the shelf under where there had once been a mirror and walked out again and stood by the door. When The Chinaman came out, Frank went back in.

I followed Frank past Bebop's counter down the stairs and into the parking lot next to the Villa Girgenti. We kicked some grimy snow out of the way and squatted down and lit up, then leaned back against the garage door as we smoked.

When we went back into the pool hall Bebop was on the phone, scratching furiously under the back of his Cub cap while threatening to kick somebody's head in, an easy thing to do over the phone. The Chinaman was sitting against the wall watching The Pole lose at eight ball. As we passed him on our way to the number nine table he nodded without moving his eyes.

"He's pretty cool," I said.

"He has to be," said Frank. "He's a Chinaman."

FIFTEEN

Around the time we were hanging out at Bebop's Pool Hall, Magic Frank decided that Tiny Majeski, a three-hundred-pound oaf who owned a record store on Western Avenue called Tiny's, had mistreated a customer, namely Frank. Frank claimed Tiny had thrown him out of the store for no good reason. "I was browsing," said Frank. "There's no law against browsing, especially when I hadn't even stole anything yet."

Frank wanted to teach Tiny a lesson, so he made up a bunch of signs, like the ones strikers carry, saying, "TINY UNFAIR TO KIDS," "TINY IS A SLOB," and "TINY IS A FAT ROTUND BUFFOON," things like that, gave them to a few of us, and asked us to help him picket Tiny's record shop. During the half hour or so we blocked the entrance to Tiny's, not one customer went in and we were having a great time, joking and yelling insults at Tiny until the cop showed up.

The first thing the cop did was whack Magic Frank on the shoulder with his billy club, rip the sign out of his hands, and spit in his face. "You crummy punks get moving," he yelled. This cop was a small, mean guy who later got thrown off the force for taking bribes or stealing stuff out of somebody's basement, something like that, I never got the whole story. I don't know how he stacked up against big-time hoods but he was great at beating up kids. He pulled out his gun and lined us all up against the wall of the bank next door. Then he got on the radio of his police car and called for a wagon. "You scumbag punks are gonna go to the can," he snarled. He was very good at snarling, he even spit while he did it.

There were five of us lined up against the wall while he waved his revolver around and grinned at the crowd. We each took off so fast in five different directions that he didn't have time to quit grinning. He started yelling and shooting into the air but he didn't know which way to go first, so he just stood there screaming at us to stop. Some crazy old guy who was sweeping his steps ran after Tex Kelly yelling, "I'll get him, Officer!" but he tripped over the wire border of his lawn and fell down.

I cut down an alley and made it all the way home with no problem. Magic Frank later told me that he and Marvin Ledbetter jumped a fence into a backyard when they saw a cop car turn into the alley they were cutting across and knocked furiously at the back door of the house. When a little old Jewish lady answered the door Frank told her that he and Marvin were frightened Jewish boys being chased by the Catholic kids from St. Tim's and would she please let them in so they wouldn't get beaten up. The lady invited them in and gave them milk and cookies, which they sat calmly eating and drinking while the cops chased around the neighborhood looking for them. They didn't leave her house until after dark and didn't have any trouble.

None of us got caught, even though the cops stopped every boy on the street around Tiny's for an hour after we'd escaped.

"I heard about that crap you guys pulled over at Tiny's," Bebop said the next day. "Some tough punks you are."

"What are you talkin' about," said Frank, "that wasn't us. We don't know who it was."

Bebop snorted and dribbled down his chin. "Tough guys," he said.

"How'd the Cubs do?" I asked him.

"What do you think?" Bebop said. "They lost. They're a bigger bunch of bums than you guys."

SIXTEEN

The next two seasons were like heaven for Cub fans. In both 1958 and '59 the Cubs finished fifth, tying for that distinction with St. Louis and Cincinnati respectively. These were the greatest years of Ernie Banks, who became the only player to win the Most Valuable Player award while playing for a second-division team two years running. In '58 Banks batted .313, hit 47 home runs, and had 129 RBI; in '59 the figures were .304, 45, and an incredible 143 RBI.

Scheffing got a few of the horses he needed: Al Dark, who batted .295, was obtained early in '58 from the Cards (for Jim Brosnan) to play third; Bobby Thomson, "the Flying Scot," home run hero of the Giants' '51 play-off victory, was picked up and placed in center; and the farm system came up with Sammy Taylor behind the plate, Tony Taylor at second base, and Glen Hobbie on the hill.

In 1958 veteran outfielder Lee Walls smacked 24 homers and made the All-Star team; Moose Moryn hit 26 out of the park, including three in a doubleheader in front of his mother, the first time she'd ever seen him play. Bill Henry, a left-handed pitcher obtained from the Red Sox, shored up the relief corps, teaming with right-hander Don Elston, who led the league in appearances with 69. It was during the '58 season, too, that the relief crew, in an effort to relieve boredom rather than a fellow pitcher in mound distress, instead caused distress to Mexican rookie hurler Marcelino Solis, whom they locked in the bullpen after a road

The Banks power swing, fashioned after the swing of Hank Thompson during softball days. (Wide World)

game. Soon after this incident Solis disappeared from the bigs. One assumes his departure was due more to his 6.06 ERA than his reaction to the schoolboy prank perpetrated by his Cub teammates.

Nineteen fifty-eight was the first of seven Opening Days at Wrigley Field that I attended on consecutive years with my friend Big Steve. Bob Anderson was the starting pitcher for one of these April openers and there was snow piled up against the outfield walls. Don Drysdale pitched for the Dodgers, who won, and hit a home run into the left-field seats. It was that year that Big Steve began to assert himself as a spokesman for the right-center-field bleacher fans. We *always* sat in the bleachers, which I still believe to be the best seats in the house—from center you can see where each pitch is and have a full view of the field—and they're still the cheapest, too. In those days it cost seventy-five cents to get into the bleachers, and that was anyone, child or adult. It was sixty-five cents for anyone fourteen or under to get into the grandstand. We disdained the boxes altogether. In fact, the only time I can remember sitting in a box seat as a kid was that one time in the Schenley liquor seats with my dad in 1952.

One game I attended with Big Steve in '58 or '59 taught me a lesson I've never forgotten: *never leave a game before it's over* (something I've done only once since, to my great and inevitable dismay). The Cubs were playing the Braves, and in the fourth inning a huge rain- and thunderstorm descended upon the stadium. I waited under the stands with Steve for over an hour. When the rain did not show any sign of letting up, I decided to leave. Steve stayed. I was on the bus near my house when the sun came out. I hurried inside, turned on the television, and wound up watching the rest of the game that way. It lasted 14 innings and Al Dark won it for the Cubs with a grand-slam home run.

The 1959 season was a glorious repeat of '58. Tony Taylor hit .280, fielded spectacularly, scored 96 runs while batting second in the lineup, two spots ahead of Banks, three in front of the new center fielder, George Altman. Big George was a left-handed slugger whose presence forced Thomson to left and resulted in Moryn and Walls sharing the third outfield spot. Altman was expected to supply some power in the order behind Banks, who was again the big gun, but a pleasant surprise was pitcher Glen Hobbie, a big, strong kid who won 16 games, including 3 shutouts, and promised to be the real thing, a consistent winner. The Elston-Henry righty-lefty bullpen tandem was effective and as balanced as possible: both men appeared in 65 games; Henry had 9 wins, Elston 10; both lost 8. There were some bum arms on the staff, like Art Ceccarelli and Johnny Buzhardt (who, like Moe Drabowsky, went on to '60s stardom as a relief pitcher in the American League—with the White Sox!), but all in all, things were looking up. After all, the White Sox had won their first flag in forty years. Anything could happen—next year it might be the Cubs' time at last.

The only real sore point of the '59 season occurred when the Cubs were not even on the field. It happened, in fact, after the season was over, during the pennant play-off between L.A. and Milwaukee. In that two-game series Braves third baseman Ed Mathews hit a home run in a losing cause, his 46th of the year, which gave him the championship by one over Ernie Banks, with whom he'd ended the regular season in a tie. Banks, of course, was not afforded the opportunity of playing in any extra games, and so had what would have been his share of a second consecutive crown unfairly snatched from him. Banks and Mathews both ended their careers with 512 homers, but to me, because of that extra shot provided and taken advantage of by Mathews, Banks takes precedence on the all-time list.

SEVENTEEN

When I was twelve I played in an important game in Little League baseball. Whichever team won the game would be in the play-offs. My team wasn't very good, but somehow we'd managed to get to that point, and the team we were playing was the previous year's champions.

Harvey, a kid I had known and disliked since first grade, was pitching for them. He was a left-hander and he'd shut out our team through the first six innings—we played only seven-inning games. I had gotten the only hit off of him, a bunt single on a three and nothing count in the first inning. Harvey was afraid to let me hit. He knew I could hit him, and he'd tried to walk me in the first but I had surprised him by bunting and beaten it out. My next two times up, the catcher interfered by tipping my bat, giving me a free pass to first base. I knew he'd done it on purpose, to keep me from hitting against Harvey, and I was furious.

I was the star hitter of my team and I was expected to get us some runs, so it had been a particularly frustrating game. Harvey's team had three runs. It was the bottom of the seventh inning, our last chance, and I stole second base. Then I stole third. Unnerved, Harvey walked the next two batters.

He was afraid of losing his shutout now, not to mention the game. Even though there were two outs, I figured we had a good chance to score. Harvey was nervous and I kept taunting him from third base. Then I saw who was up: Alvie Weinstock, the worst hitter on the team, if not the worst hitter in the entire league. I couldn't believe it. The coach, in an apparent effort to be "fair," to give everyone a chance to play, had pinch-hit Weinstock for our pitcher, who was not a bad hitter. I knew why he'd done it, though: Alvie Weinstock's father was an assistant coach on our team.

I yelled at the coach, "Let Goodman hit! Let Goodman bat for himself!" But he wouldn't listen.

Before Weinstock knew what had happened, Harvey'd slipped two strikes across the plate. There was no doubt that Weinstock was going to strike out, we'd lose, it would be the end of the season, and hated Harvey would have pitched a one-hit shutout. It was all too much for me to take. I took a long lead off of third base.

"Hey, Harvey, hey, hey," I yelled.

Harvey looked over at me. All he had to do was throw one more pitch to Weinstock and it would be all over. I dared him to try and pick me off. I was counting on Harvey's vanity, and it worked—Harvey threw over to the third baseman, lazily, just to keep me close. I broke for home on the dead run.

Everybody was screaming. I yelled at Weinstock to block the catcher, to step in front of him, get in his way so that I could score. Instead, Weinstock stepped back, out of the box. The catcher, who was smart—remember he'd tipped my bat twice—and good, blocked the plate. I was out by ten feet.

All of the coaches stormed around me while I lay there. I wasn't anywhere near the plate.

Mr. Weinstock was yelling down at me. "You're incorrigible!" he shouted—he didn't like me anyway. "You're a delinquent!" He was louder than anyone.

"Alvie would have struck out," I said to him. "I wanted to break the shutout."

My stepfather was there. He'd come to pick me up after the game and had seen what had happened. Mr. Weinstock started yelling at him.

"Does he listen at home? He's no good, that kid, no good, I tell you. He doesn't follow orders. He's gonna end up no good."

My stepfather didn't like me much either, but he didn't give a damn about baseball, and he wasn't stupid—at least, not stupid enough to get carried away by a twelve-year-old's baseball game —so he didn't say anything. Then the coach came over.

"I'm not going to let you play in the All-Star game because of that stunt," he said to me, although he later relented because I was the only one on the team chosen to play and he wanted the team to be represented.

I began taking off my spikes, changing into my regular shoes. Harvey came over.

"Nice try," he said.

"Fuck you," I said.

Then my stepfather and I drove home.

"How was the game?" my mother asked.

When I didn't say anything she looked at my stepfather for an answer.

"They lost," he told her.

"Oh, that's too bad. You must be disappointed," she said to me.

"Yes," I said.

"Well then," she said, "I'll leave you alone."

I thanked her and went into my room.

"He's so sensitive," I heard her say to my stepfather before I closed the door.

EIGHTEEN

It was about this time—1959—that Big Steve and I began in professional earnest (the loser paid for however many bottles of soda pop the winner could drink after the game) our rivalry in a contest known in the neighborhood as "Fastball Pitching," or, more colloquially, just "Fastball."

The game ritual began at Walsh's Drugstore on Washtenaw where we each chipped in a quarter toward the purchase of two white baseball-like rubber balls. Locally, only Walsh's carried the correct kind of rubber ball with upraised imitation stitches to aid one's grip upon it. This particular ball, which we called a Walshball, held up better, longer, than any other rubber ball. Tennis balls, besides being too small, cut too readily and were too easy to curve and dip. Only Walshballs had that necessary heft in the hand similar to a regular hardball.

We played at the grammar school, where divisions along one wall had been conveniently delineated by the builder in 1910 or whenever it was the school was built. These divided areas, defined by outcroppings of brick at regular intervals, established at least six fastball lanes. Often that many games were being played at one time. A box approximating the normal strike zone —a foot wide, shoulders to knees—was marked heavily in chalk on the wall, and a pitcher's line was drawn in the gravel about forty or forty-five feet from the wall. Batters' boxes were outlined in the gravel by the bat handle on either side of the chalked strike rectangle. A pitch in the box was a strike—the pitcher called all

The author in 1959
(Courtesy of Barry Gifford)

pitches—as was a liner. The batter, of course, could protest what he considered questionable calls, and if he was adamant enough the pitch had to be taken over again.

A ball hit in the air that bounced past the pitcher's line up to the second tree along the sidewalk that ran parallel to the field was a single; past the second tree was a double; off the fence—which was about two hundred feet away—was a triple; over it was a homer. A ball caught by the pitcher either on a fly or off the first bounce was an out, as were ground balls. A grounder taken by the pitcher on one hop could be called a double play if, of course, there were fewer than two outs, and applied only to a runner attempting to advance from first to second base; no runners advancing to third or home could be doubled up or called out as part of a double play. No bunting was allowed.

The side boundaries were defined by the line of trees along the sidewalk on the right and the end of the building on the left;

if you were playing in the middle lane, about forty feet in each direction from the center of the field. Obviously, the definition of the playing area heavily favored the hitter who could resist pulling the ball. When later I played in Pony League, high school and college, I was particularly adept at hitting singles through the pitcher's box and out over second base, a skill I attributed directly to the confined area necessary to batting successfully in fastball. Any fly ball hit beyond the boundaries on either side was a foul ball. If caught by the pitcher on the fly or one bounce, it was an out.

Though we often played other opponents, Big Steve and I carried on a personal series that superseded in importance those contests. We played more than sixty games a year, which probably explains why by the time I was seventeen my arm had pretty well lost its elasticity. My fast ball was at its peak when I was fifteen; after that I relied mainly on curves, an occasional slider, and, when it worked, a hooking sinker that was unhittable but more often than not out of the strike zone. Still, it looked good coming up there and it was my most reliable out pitch on Big Steve.

As a pitcher Big Steve was far superior to me. He was much faster and threw a heavy ball which, when Big Steve was on and the batter could hit the ball, forced him to hit it on the ground. He also had a back-up pitch that he'd learned from watching White Sox pitcher Dick Donovan demonstrate his technique on television. This pitch threw off a batter's timing—it came in hard, like a fast ball, only because Steve would leave a wider space between his palm and the ball, and because of the particular grip he put on it, even though his release was the same exact motion as he used to throw a fast ball, the pitch—if it worked properly —would seem to hesitate a fraction just at that point before the batter where, if it were a fast ball, it would explode on him. At that moment the ball would die a little (because of the particular turn it took) and the batter (me), expecting the fast ball, would have to try to slow up his swing in order to meet the pitch properly and get good wood on the ball. This was Big Steve's pop-up pitch, and I never could hit it with any consistency. Only when he turned it over the wrong way, or released it too high in his motion, could I adjust quickly enough to hit it on a line.

Big Steve's most potent weapon, however, was his knockdown pitch. He never hesitated to throw at a batter's head. The Walshball was rubber but it hurt when it tagged you at eighty or ninety miles per hour in the back or arm. Once in Little League, Steve, who was a star pitcher, told the coach of a rival team, who had once cut Steve from the squad both because he didn't like Steve's attitude and to make room for his own son, that if the son came up to bat against him Steve would hit him in the head—and this was hard ball, not Walshball. The coach did send his son up to bat as a pinch hitter late in the game, after Big Steve's team had it locked, and, of course, Steve steamed a pitch right at the kid's head. The coach's son, however, threw up his left arm and caught the ball on the elbow. Big Steve didn't even wait to be thrown out of the game, he just walked right off the field and away. "It slipped," was all he would say.*

Steve was a great competitor. I've always thought of him as Billy Martin's kind of player. He could hit, too, and for power, especially to the opposite field; but he couldn't run at all. Even before he hurt his knees in high school and had to have extensive operations on each one, he was extremely slow. (I was with him the evening he broke all of the little bones behind his right knee by stepping into a hole in the alley while we were playing ball —his body twisted completely around except for his right leg— and I could hear the crack.) Steve's lack of foot was due partially to his weight—he weighed two hundred pounds in eighth grade (he was then already about five feet ten inches tall), but mostly it was because his legs were so short, like Philly slugger Greg "the Bull" Luzinski's. His legs were very powerful but stubby, and no matter how hard he tried he just couldn't cover ground with anything resembling decent speed.

(Big Steve never walked, he shuffled. He was very proud of the fact that he wore out a new pair of shoes every month. Once

---

*The pitch broke the kid's arm.

---

his mother bought him a pair of super-tough Boy Scout shoes which he managed to shred in six weeks, a record for durability. Steve even thought of doing an ad for the manufacturer: "Hi, I'm Big Steve. For me a new pair of shoes lasts a month, sometimes less. These Boy Scout jobs made it through almost six weeks of football, baseball, basketball in the alley, and general shuffling. The way I do it, just the shuffling is usually enough to do in a new pair in no time. Think what these Boy Scout babies will do for you. Try 'em out, and tell your local shoe store guy Big Steve sent ya.")

One year we played a World Series that, except for one game, was even all the way to the seventh game. I'd beaten Steve badly that one time—12 to 4, I think the score was—because he'd faded in the unseasonable hundred-degree heat. It was close up to the fifth or sixth inning when Steve wilted and couldn't get the fast ball by me. I can still remember teeing off on it that day; triples and homers flew off my bat seemingly without effort on my part. That one game almost made up for all those others Steve had me beaten before the fifth inning. He had to quit in the seventh, and we went to the gas station on Rosemont where we bought the bottles of pop out of an old lift-top cooler for a nickel apiece. We each drank about six bottles of orange and grape Nehi that day while we sat inside the station waiting room next to the fan reading old issues of *Sports Illustrated* and *Sport*. That was the day I read about Willie McCovey's debut with the San Francisco Giants (July 30, 1959), when he went 4 for 4, 2 triples and 2 singles, at old Seals Stadium, and I felt as if I'd done just as well as Willie that day, maybe better.

But the seventh game of our private Series was a different story. We played after school with several other kids watching, so we were both particularly up for it. The game came down to the bottom of the ninth with Big Steve up by one run. I was up with the bases loaded and two away. Steve went into his fast ball motion, I guessed backup pitch, held back for the fade, and then met it perfectly. I can still hear the sock of that rubber Walshball on the bat. Unbelievably, just as Tommy Hayden had caught my line drive by throwing up his glove hand to protect himself, Steve snagged the shot off my bat in the web of his glove for the third out. At first he didn't even know where the ball was. When I yelled in pain and disbelief he looked at his mitt and shuffled in.

When Steve got in to where I was standing, still in shock from seeing my sure hit turned into the final out, the bat at my feet where I'd dropped it, he knocked into me with his shoulder the way he always did when he was feeling good—and still does whenever we meet after not having seen one another for a long time—and grinned. "Had it all the way," he said.

NINETEEN

In the winter of 1959–60 the Cubs did themselves a terrific disservice by dealing away Tony Taylor, who, with Philadelphia and Detroit, would wind up playing 19 big league seasons, amassing over 2,000 hits, and becoming at the tail end of his career one of the premier pinch hitters in baseball history, rapping 17 pinch safeties in 1974 alone.

Other than an unsuccessful experiment with an eighteen-year-old left-handed hitting outfielder named Danny Murphy (9 hits in 75 at bats for a .120 average and no power), the most noteworthy occurrence of the 1960 Cub season was a trade, not of players and not even between two teams, but the exchange, 17 games into the season, of Lou Boudreau, who was working as one of the Cubs' radio broadcasters, for Charlie Grimm, who had begun the campaign as the managerial successor to Bob Scheffing. (Scheffing resurfaced in 1961 as pilot of the Detroit Tigers, who finished second that season.)

Boudreau, of course, had previously managed Cleveland (when he was only twenty-four years old), Boston, and Kansas City, all American League teams, most notably his Indian outfit of 1948, which won the World Series that season, a year in which Boudreau, as full-time shortstop as well as manager, had batted .355 and driven in 106 runs. He even *caught* in one game for the Tribe that year.

Grimm, known jocularly around the league as "Jolly Cholly," perhaps became more famous for playing his banjo on the radio during dull moments (and they were numerous) in the games than he had as a player or manager. Jolly Cholly had managed the Cubs with fair success in the '30s and '40s, twice winning the pennant and three times finishing second, and the Braves in the early '50s, finishing second twice and third once in five years.

In 1960, however, though he'd had bad clubs before, I guess the prospect of feeling even partially responsible for what was bound to be a dismal business was too much for Grimm to contemplate for long. When Boudreau agreed to the switch—the first recorded case of a club's radio broadcaster taking over the manager's reins, preceeding San Diego's Jerry Coleman by twenty years—Jolly Cholly happily agreed to assist Jack Quinlan in the radio booth.

Boudreau, who by this time was not merely the new Cub pilot but Detroit pitcher Denny McLain's father-in-law, must have early on sensed that his presence wasn't about to make a bit of difference to the team. The Cubs wound up one game from the cellar, with a record of 60 wins and 94 losses. Only Philadelphia was worse, a fact Phillie manager Eddie Sawyer caught on to even before Jolly Cholly's revelation in Chicago. Sawyer quit his job as manager in the City of Brotherly Love after only *one* game into the 1960 season, not relishing the thought of being on hand for a third consecutive cellar finish. The day he quit, Sawyer said that the Phillies were hopeless, he couldn't win with what the owners had given him to work with, and that third baseman Ted Lepcio, whom Philadelphia had obtained over the winter from the Tigers, was the single worst player he'd seen in his baseball career.

The few bright spots of the Cub season were, as always, Ernie Banks, who beat out Aaron and Mathews for the home run crown with 41 to their 40 and 39 respectively, becoming the only shortstop in National League history to lead the league in both home runs and fielding, while also driving in 117 runs; and Richie Ashburn, the veteran Phillie star center fielder who came over in the Tony Taylor deal and hit .291. Ron Santo made his debut at third base; Ed Bouchee, who was having a variety of personal

Ernie Banks
(Courtesy of Barry Gifford)

problems during this time, took over at first; and Frank Thomas, obtained from Cincinnati, hit 21 homers as a part-time performer. Glen Hobbie, who was expected to win 20 games, *lost* 20 while winning 16; and Don Elston, determined to use his newly acquired knuckle ball, watched his ERA rise in direct proportion to the soaring shots opposing batters hit off the knuckler. Moe Thacker and Sammy Taylor, the catchers, hit for a combined average of below .200. There was little for Wrigley Field fans to cheer.

The 1960 World Series was the greatest post-season classic I've ever seen, with Pittsburgh, having won *their* first pennant in thirty-five years, edging the Yankees 10 to 9 in one of the most exciting seventh games in Series history. (I was in Japan in 1975, so missed the Cincinnati-Boston confrontation that October, a Series widely considered to have been the equal of the 1960 battle.) New York scored 55 runs and still lost. Whitey Ford pitched 2 shutouts, Bobby Richardson batted in 12 runs, and Mickey Mantle hit 3 homers, but none of it was enough as Pirate second baseman Bill Mazeroski stroked a home run in the bottom of the ninth in the final game to earn eternal fame and glory.

As I walked home from a friend's house after watching the seventh game of the World Series on TV, it occurred to me that because the Cubs seemed not to expect to win when they were on the field, that was why, or part of the reason why they did not. I'd noticed this business of attitude earlier in the season during a game the Cubs had played against the Reds. Cincinnati, though they were not a particularly outstanding team, *looked* confident out there. Not just their great players like Frank Robinson and Vada Pinson, the others, too, at least appeared *hopeful*. On the Cubs, only Ernie Banks seemed cheerful and he was the only one doing anything worth mentioning. I began to realize that it might be a long wait before I would have the privilege of watching the Cubs do anything after the regular season other than pack their bags.

TWENTY

In 1960, the Cubs, despite fifth-place finishes in the previous two years, were not drawing many fans. So few people attended Cub games in those days that Wally Phillips, a local television and radio personality who then did a pregame TV show called "Fan in the Stand," wound up interviewing Big Steve two days in a row. Phillips's job was to do a five-minute interview with a fan in a different part of the ball park each day before the game began, and one day he chose Steve for the interview. The next afternoon Steve was back at the park for a game with the Phillies, the only team to lose more games in the National League that season than the Cubs, and there couldn't have been more than five hundred people in the park including ushers, vendors, players, reporters, and the grounds crew. Big Steve went up to Wally Phillips just prior to his going on the air and said, "Well, here I am." "I just interviewed you yesterday," said Wally. "I can't have you on the show twice in a row." Steve laughed. "See anybody else around?" he asked. He was right, there wasn't one other fan in the section of seats where they were standing, so Phillips went ahead and let Steve do the show.

Steve was also on another show where he talked about the Cubs. It was an early-evening Saturday show called "The First Freedom." Volunteers would come on camera and talk for three minutes about anything they wanted to. It was videotaped, so there was no guarantee they'd be on when the program was aired a week or two later, but Steve made it and I didn't.

"The First Freedom" was taped outdoors on State Street in the Loop, in front of the State & Lake theater. I went on first and talked about some "important" (I thought at the time) political topic. Then Steve got on and talked about the Cubs, calling Ron Santo (who'd just joined the team) a bum, castigating Cub Vice-President John Holland for trading Tony Taylor, telling the Cub brass they should pay Ernie Banks more money, and so on. While Steve was on the air a religious pamphleteer accosted me and offered me six dollars to go home with him.

When "our" segment of "The First Freedom" ran the following week, there was Steve, big as ever, bellowing about the Cubs. I didn't get a word in, and Steve was by far the star of the show. Not only was he good on camera but, as he told me later, the show's producer had told him right after he'd been taped that he'd be on for sure. When Steve asked him if I'd be on, too, the producer had said probably not. I'd done all right, he told Steve, but Chicago viewers weren't interested in that intellectual stuff.

"How come you chose the Cubs to talk about?" I asked Steve after the program ran.

"It was a sure thing," he said. "Everyone has a beef about the Cubs."

TWENTY-ONE

Aside from the Boudreau-Grimm dugout/broadcast booth switch, the outstanding Cub event of 1960 was newly acquired pitcher Don Cardwell's no-hitter on Sunday, May 15. He threw it in the second game of a doubleheader that I'll never forget because I left, along with Big Steve, after the first game.

Cardwell was a tall right-hander who hadn't done much in three seasons with the Phillies, and whose best season out of an eventual total of 14 would be his next, 1961, when he would win 15 for the Cubs. But he had potential, and wasn't old, and the Cubs didn't have much else to offer. A new face was something, anyway, and we were eager to see how he'd do. After so many seasons of more forgettable arms than I'd care to look up in *The Baseball Encyclopedia*, in 1960 Don Cardwell appeared to us as a dim ray of hope.

There was an unusually large crowd at Wrigley Field that sunny May Sunday, and the Cubs lost the first game despite some heroics by Ernie Banks. Steve and I couldn't stay for the second game, we had to go to a wedding party, so we took a bus to his house, where we changed clothes, and walked to Maureen Ainsley's. Maureen's father, who looked exactly like Stan Musial, was to drive us to the hotel where the party would be taking place.

Cardwell was pitching the second game as scheduled—his first appearance in a Cub uniform—and after seven innings, Mr. Ainsley told us when we got to his house, Cardwell had a no-hitter going. At least I hadn't broken the promise I'd made to myself following the game Al Dark had won with a grand slam in the fourteenth inning never to leave a game in progress (that heinous transgression would come much later)—I'd left *before* Cardwell toed the rubber for the first official heave.

The closest I'd come to seeing a no-hitter performed in person was 5 2/3 perfect innings by Robin Roberts for Philadelphia vs. the Cubs the year before. Seeing Larsen's perfect Series win on TV wasn't the same as *being* there, and I knew I'd feel terrible for having left if Cardwell came through, which, of course, he did.

On the way to the hotel we listened to the game on Mr. Ainsley's car radio. By the time we got there it was the ninth inning and we stayed in the car and listened to Cardwell retire the last three Cardinal batters. So we missed the big moment, and I promised myself then that I'd never again leave a game *before* it started, either.

Unfortunately, on August 24, 1975, I broke that initial promise to myself for the first and only time. Again I was at a doubleheader, this time at Candlestick Park in San Francisco, the Giants vs. the Mets. The Mets won the first contest handily as Dave Kingman, whom the Giants had sold to New York earlier in the year, belted a single and a home run to lead the way. Ed Halicki was scheduled to start the second game for the Giants; he was then in his second season and hadn't done much to distinguish himself, but my friend Richard, with whom I'd driven to the park, kept telling me what a fine pitcher Halicki was, that he was one of the best young hurlers in the league. Halicki had pitched passably or better on a few occasions but he'd been banged around plenty in between. I had promised an old friend that I would attend a party she was giving late that afternoon (since I was not much of a social-gathering type, it was practically the first party of any kind I'd attended since that wedding in 1960), and I told Richard I had to leave after a few innings of the second game, that someone would be meeting me in a car outside the ball park at four o'clock.

After four innings Halicki had a no-hitter. The game was pretty dull, though, there hadn't been any really tough fielding plays; it looked as it always does when a pitcher is completely on, as if the Mets were barely able to stand up straight at the plate. At four o'clock I got up to leave. "He won't pitch a no-hitter," I said to Richard. "Halicki's good, but he's not that good."

I went to the party, which was terrible and a waste of time, but I was afraid to turn on a radio to find out what had happened in the game. Nobody at the party knew or cared anything about baseball; when I mentioned to one of the other guests that Halicki had been working on a no-hitter when I'd left, he stared blankly and said, "Oh?"

On my way home that night there was an accident on the freeway that held traffic up interminably. As the car inched along, it began to rain and I broke down and switched on the radio. Halicki's no-hitter was the highlight of the news.

Twice in one still-young lifetime.

As Richard said to me later, "Perhaps you're caught up in a syndrome of some kind, but if I were you I'd try not to think about it too much."

TWENTY-TWO

Green Briar Park, bounded by Peterson, Washtenaw, Talman, and Glenlake streets, consisted of a baseball and football field (sans goalposts) encircled by magnificent Dutch elm trees, a concrete outdoor basketball court with chain-net baskets, and a field house.

There were baseball games at GB, as the park was called, every clear day from April until the first snow. We played softball only, not hardball, with a sixteen-inch "Clincher" and no gloves. Balls hit into the overhanging trees were usually playable if caught—if the tree interfered with a player's catching a ball, and it dropped to the ground, it was considered a foul ball; if it was caught before hitting the ground, the batter was out.

Kids of all ages played ball at GB, even guys who'd graduated or dropped out of high school. One famous regular was Chuck Syracuse, a crazy kid who'd been thrown out of school at the age of nineteen, in his third year of high school, and spent every day at GB playing softball. At night he drove a cab. One afternoon Syracuse came by in his cab, got out to watch the game for a few minutes—he needed extra money, he said, so that week he was working days, too—and after an inning or so somebody left and Chuck took his place. It was a high-scoring game that went into extra innings, it took a long time to play, and when Syracuse got back to his taxi he discovered that he'd left the meter running. He went berserk and began beating on the roof of the cab. Finally he got in and drove away.

A few days later—during which time Chuck had not shown up at GB—we found out that Syracuse had turned the cab over in an empty lot in another neighborhood and torched it, then told the cab company that it had been stolen while he was eating lunch. The company didn't buy his story and investigated the case. When they confronted him with the truth he told them he'd done it so that he wouldn't be charged the thirty-five bucks run up on the meter while he'd been playing softball at the park.

Since Chuck couldn't pay the three or four grand the company said he owed them for the cab, he did a little time at Joliet. After he got out of the joint Chuck continued to hang out at GB, where he suddenly found himself a famous person. He spent more time answering questions about his insane torch job than playing softball. One day Magic Frank was kidding around and asked Syracuse if he thought he'd handled the situation properly.

"What do you mean?" Chuck asked.

"Do you think it was worth it?" said Frank.

"Well," said Syracuse, thinking it over a bit, "you know I went four for five in the game that day."

TWENTY-THREE

GB was the scene of a number of legendary neighborhood athletic contests, none more so than the 1960 local grammar school league basketball championship. The old brown field house contained some upstairs meeting rooms that were used by the Girl Scouts and Campfire Girls, and downstairs a large, drafty hall for VFW smokers, and a basketball court. Though it was full-court, it wasn't high school regulation, so only grammar school and club ball games were played there.

I was on that '59–'60 team for Clinton School, and we had a couple of good players, the best of whom were Bob "The Beef" Bufante, who was six feet tall and 220 pounds and couldn't be stopped inside—not that he always put the ball in the basket, but he'd bash anybody out of his way—and little Sid "The Destroyer" Guglielmi, a cousin of the great Notre Dame and Washington Redskin quarterback Ralph Guglielmi. Sid had a deadly ten-foot jumper but couldn't make a lay-up. The rest of us put the ball up with far less certainty as to where it might come down, so we left most of the scoring to them. The league champions that year were to receive a dozen free tickets apiece to Cub games the following summer. Some kids felt this was a rather dubious prize to be playing for, but the main thing was to win the league, for pride if not for the Cub tickets. (Actually, it would have been a more attractive prize had it been possible at least to *sell* the tickets.)

The star of the league was Stone School's center Jimmy

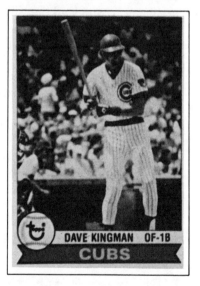

(Courtesy of Barry Gifford)

Athens, who, it was rumored, was fifteen years old. The league age limit was fourteen, though all of the players I knew were twelve or thirteen. Athens certainly looked older than the other boys. He was six-one, about 170, and shaved every other day. He was also left-handed, which confused most kids whose job it was to guard him, his specialty being an eight-foot three-quarter hook from the middle of the free-throw lane.

That year both Clinton and Stone came into the championship game undefeated, though Stone's margin of victory in each game had been approximately twice that of Clinton's. We had been lucky to beat Boone School, a team I considered better than us, 20 to 16, while Stone, with Athens scoring all but 6 of their points, ran over them 52 to 12. With only thirty-two minutes of running time in which to play, 52 points was an astronomical figure, and Jimmy Athens's 46 was a GB field house record.*

Our only chance was to stall, to keep possession of the ball until we could lay in a cripple, then collapse three men on Athens and hope for the best. The week of the game we practiced our perimeter passing and the Wildcat Weave we'd seen Northwestern work, but none of us, except for Bob the Beef, thought we had a prayer. The Beef didn't like the stall strategy. He put up with it during practice but told me privately that he had his own game plan. I rarely doubted the Beef's ability to handle a situation, but it was going to take something special to contain Jimmy Athens.

The night before the game Bufante and I were hanging out in front of Mama Valentino's pizza place on Touhy Avenue when Norm Skikorsky grabbed some guy he was laying for just as the guy came out the door of Mama's, and slit his throat. I couldn't believe Skikorsky had done it—I mean Norm was an animal, and I'd heard about some crazy stuff he'd pulled, but hearing about that kind of thing and seeing some guy barf blood all over the snow out of a hole in his throat that's not supposed

---

*This record was broken by Steve Fagin, a maniacal Cub and Cincinnati Bearcat fan, who scored 54.

---

to be there are two very different things. The Beef, who wasn't afraid of anything, came to his senses first. "Let's go," he said to me, and we took off like Little Looie and Big Klu.

The Skikorsky stabbing was the big news the next day at the game. Apparently the guy he'd sliced wasn't dead, which was hard to believe, but he was in the hospital. Norm the Animal was hiding out someplace. It was tough for me to keep my mind on the game, but to the surprise of all of us, the stall worked. The Beef bumped Athens on the tip, got away with it, and we managed to keep the ball for eight minutes—the entire first quarter—without allowing a basket. We didn't get one either, but we couldn't have been more confident coming out for the second period. The Clinton fans lined up against the walls—there wasn't any room for chairs, only benches for the teams—were cheering and shouting abuse at Athens, asking him if he'd shaved that day and who he'd voted for in the last election.

Athens didn't jump for Stone in the second quarter. At the last second he lined up on the side opposite the Beef, and before he could stop himself Bufante tapped the ball right to Athens, who dribbled straight in to the basket and scored the first two points of the game. We held the ball when we got it and lost it only twice, both times to Athens, who hooked it in once from the left side of the lane and the other time passed it off on a fast break to Donny Rademaker, their quick little guard, who beat everybody downcourt for a lay-up. But that was it for the half, and it ended with Stone leading 6 to nothing.

Sitting in the locker room, I asked the Beef when he was going to spring his strategy. He popped a pimple on his neck, stared at the pus on his finger, rubbed it off on his shorts, stood up, and looked down at me. "I'll use it," he said, and turned away. "I got to go take a leak."

Athens hooked in two more in the third period, but the Destroyer, unable to contain himself any longer, popped in two from the outside for us, our first points, and we went into the final quarter trailing 10 to 4.

Early in the period Sid stole the ball from Rademaker and blew an easy lay-up, but it caromed directly into the Beef's hands and he banked it home to cut Stone's lead to 4. As we headed downcourt after the basket there was a scream from the fans, and when I looked back Sid was leaping up and down clapping his hands. He'd stolen the in-bounds pass and made a lay-up, practically the first of his life, leaving us only two points back.

Stone called a time-out and came out afterward in a stall of their own. They figured they could hold the ball for the last six minutes and not risk a shot unless Athens was open under the hoop. As the clock ticked down to the final minute the kids lined alongside the court screamed louder and louder, and then, with thirty seconds to go, the Beef picked up Jimmy Athens, who had the ball, and held him over his head. The referee blew his whistle and shouted, "Foul! Foul!" but the Beef wouldn't drop Athens until the ref, who was about six inches shorter than the Beef, began hacking at his arms.

The Beef was thrown out of the game and Athens was awarded a foul shot. The fans were wild and the Beef paraded over with his fists raised in the victory sign and stood with them, keeping his arms up in the air.

A substitute replaced the Beef and we lined up for the free throw. Athens looked stunned and upset and he missed the shot badly. Sid got the rebound and dribbled madly around, finally driving across mid-court and letting the ball fly just as the clock ran out. Incredibly, it went off the backboard and in, and when I turned to find the Destroyer I saw him lying on the floor, doubled up in pain, his hands against his stomach. The ref was blowing his whistle and pointing at Jimmy Athens, then he thumbed him out of the game. The Beef ran onto the court and punched Athens in the face, picked him up, carried him to the side of the court, and threw him against the brick wall.

None of the players moved. Jerry Rosen, the field house director, ran in with Mr. Jensen, the custodian, and dragged the Beef off Athens, who looked like a pile of rags. Mr. Jensen led the Beef away, and Jerry Rosen and the ref carried Athens over to the Stone bench and laid him down on it.

Sid got up, still bent over and holding his stomach, and told us that Athens had elbowed him in the gut just as he went up for the shot. The ref came over and blew his whistle and bounced the ball on the free-throw line. The game was tied, there was no time left, but Sid had one free throw coming as a result of the foul.

The noise stopped. Sid straightened up and took the ball. He bounced it once, took a deep breath, pumped his arms, and threw the ball in the basket, swish. We mobbed him and the Clinton fans ran onto the court and hugged and kissed the players. I looked over and saw Jimmy Athens sitting up on the Stone bench checking with his hand to see if his lip was bloody. It was.

By the time I got down to the locker room Bufante had showered and was half-dressed. We grabbed each other and hugged.

"I just heard about Skikorsky," he said. "The cops found him hiding in the basement at his cousin's over on Pulaski. He's not such a bad guy, I don't think," said the Beef, pulling his sweater over his head. "Just once in a while he gets a little too violent."

TWENTY-FOUR

By 1961 the Cubs were desperate enough to try anything, and anything turned out to be their rotating coach system as a substitute for the standard single manager. Boudreau retreated to the radio booth and the Cub brass decided to hire, not one, but several leaders for their motley assortment of brutes, each spending a few weeks at the helm. Vedie Himsl, Harry Craft, Elvin Tappe, and Lou Klein all shared skipper's duties that season, none with any success. For the record, Himsl was 10 and 21; Craft, 7 and 9; Tappe, 42 and 53; Klein, 5 and 7.

Banks, who suffered through a brief experimental tour of duty in left field, slumped slightly following his three consecutive brilliant seasons to 29 homers and 80 RBI. On the bright side, though, Big George Altman, who in the off-season had become a star for the Cienfuegos team of the Cuban League (Cuban baseball games were broadcast in Chicago late on Saturday nights by Al Helfer and his voluptuous assistant Norma, whose only job was to flip the cards showing what inning it was and whatever her decolletage would allow), became a star in the National League as well, batting .303 with 27 home runs and 96 RBI. Altman also led the National League in triples, with 12. Third baseman Santo had the first of what would become a string of All-Star quality seasons with the bat, averaging .284, with 23 homers and 83 RBI, though he led the league in errors at his position with 31.

But the biggest plus was rookie of the year Billy Williams, who established himself in left field after Banks's return to shortstop. Williams displayed his sweet, smooth southpaw swing for a .278 batting average that produced 25 home runs and 86 RBI. Williams was less than Golden Glove material in the outfield, however, leading the senior circuit with 11 errors, in particular having difficulty handling line drives hit right at him; on several occasions I witnessed his being handcuffed by those kinds of direct, tough shots. It took him some time to get comfortably acquainted with left field, but within a couple of seasons Billy had made himself into a complete player, a true all-around perennial All-Star. And of course he maintained that perfect swing. Billy Williams was perhaps the purest hitter I've ever seen.

Richie Ashburn, who shared center-field duty with Al Heist, finally began to feel his age, and his '61 average dropped to .257. Andre Rodgers, from the Bahamas, spelled Banks at short. Don "No-Hit" Cardwell led the pitching staff with 15 wins, while Glen Hobbie continued to fade, suffering much of the season from a sore arm. Dick Ellsworth, a sharp left-hander, picked up 10 victories and showed good potential. Don Elston persisted in surrendering home run balls and gave way as king of the bullpen to knuckleballer Barney Schultz, who was picked up during the off-season from Detroit. Schultz, with his 2.70 ERA in 41 games, became a favorite of Wrigley-goers.

Nineteen sixty-one was, of course, the season of Yankee outfielder Roger Maris's 61 home runs, and an expansion year for the American League. The National League would add Houston and the Mets in '62, and the joke in the Wrigley Field bleachers was that starting next year the Cubs would still finish eighth but not be in last place. In very short order this proved to be wishful thinking.

In September of 1961 the Cubs brought up from the minors a twenty-two-year-old left-handed outfielder named Lou Brock. Brock had batted .361 in his first year of organized baseball at St. Cloud in Class C, and in his first at bat in the bigs Brock bounced a single up the middle. I saw that hit and could hardly have guessed that before that particular batter was through he'd have added better than 3,000 more (3,022 more, to be exact). What I might have predicted, however, was that he'd get most of them for a team other than the Cubs.

TWENTY-FIVE

The Cub pitching staff of the early '60s was so pathetic at times that the *Chicago American*, I think it was (if not the *American*, now defunct, then one of the other Chicago newspapers of the day), advocated bringing back the old Negro League and Cleveland Indian star Satchel Paige—at least, the paper reasoned, Paige could then accumulate the final few appearances he needed to qualify for his Major League pension, and he certainly couldn't do any worse than what the Cub hurlers had perpetrated so far. Charlie Finley finally did bring Paige back in 1965 (when Satch was in his own sixties) for just that purpose; and, not incidentally, to boost the then Kansas City Athletics' sagging gate. I believe that had Bill Veeck owned the Cubs he would have done it, just as he activated Minnie Minoso on his 1976 White Sox club to guarantee Minnie an extra degree of pension provision.*Paige, by the way, started one game for the A's in '65, pitched 3 innings, gave up only one hit, struck out one, and walked none, a performance any one of the Cub pitchers of '61 would have sold his soul to have given.

It seemed preordained that the woman I would eventually marry and have children with would have some connection to Chicago and baseball—even, amazingly enough, with Satchel

---

*Veeck also activated Minoso in 1980 so that he could be a five-decade player (1940s, '50s, '60s, '70s and 80s).

Paige. Though she was born and raised in San Francisco, where I met her in 1968, Mary Lou's father was born and grew up in Chicago on North Kildare Avenue near the Bohemian National Cemetery. In his younger days he was a catcher for the touring House of David semi-pro baseball team. According to my mother-in-law, he was the only player on the team at that time without a beard. She also said he had been scouted by the St. Louis Browns and the Cubs, who apparently decided that the condition of his legs, which he'd injured playing basketball at college in Iowa, was too dubious for them to take a chance on.

His name was Cromer George Nelson, and I would love to have asked him about those House of David days, especially to hear how it felt to have batted against Satchel Paige, which Cromer had done when Satch was in his prime. Paige was fond of telling the story about how one of the House of David batters he'd faced had been awarded first base after being hit by a pitch on the tip of his long beard. Paige had argued with the umpire, to no avail, that such excessive whiskers were not an actual part of a man. "They is air," claimed Satch.

But Cro, as he was called, died when Mary Lou was eight, so I never had the chance to hear his stories first-hand. I've always assumed, however, that since he grew up on the North Side he must have been a Cub fan. One story Cro told Mary Lou's mother was that whenever his House of David team—a hard-nosed bunch of religious crusaders—played a team from the Negro Leagues, as when they faced Satchel Paige, they—the House of David—would make certain to sharpen their spikes in full view of the Negro team just before the game, to try to intimidate them. The House of David was not, however, a whites-only organization. In fact, in 1934 Satchel Paige himself pitched for them, wearing a false red beard!

TWENTY-SIX

It was while the Cubs were floundering around in or near the cellar during the late '50s and very early '60s that I discovered and read all of the Chip Hilton sports books by Clair Bee. The hero of *Touchdown Pass, Strike Three, Hoop Crazy, Pitchers' Duel, Dugout Jinx,* and twenty or more other titles, Chip Hilton, as invented by Bee, was a tall, handsome, blond-haired, gray-eyed boy in the small town of Valley Falls who was a great athlete and exemplary human being. There was nobody nicer or fairer or a more intense and dedicated athletic competitor than Chip, and I wanted to be just like him even though I had dark hair and blue eyes, wasn't particularly tall, lived in a big city, was not always nice or fair, and, even though I was a good athlete, was too often indifferent to the outcome of games in which I was playing.

Clair Bee had been a famous basketball coach at Long Island University, and the Chip Hilton series stressed sportsmanship combined with an acute knowledge of baseball, basketball, and football. Each story involved Chip in dual sporting and social dilemmas that inevitably culminated in a tension-filled but ultimately satisfying climax. There was never an unhappy ending. The overall title of Coach Bee's pantheon could just as well have been *The Gospel According to Chip Hilton.*

Chip lived with his mother, who was an operator at the Valley Falls telephone company. His father, "Big Chip," had been killed in an accident at the local pottery, where he had been foreman. My mother knew that I would have preferred her to be a little old gray-haired lady who worked at the phone company and did nothing else but keep house and care for me, and she used to tease me about it. She was a beautiful, sophisticated, relatively high-living young woman in those days, but I didn't really care because none of my friends' mothers were like Chip Hilton's mother either.

(Courtesy of Barry Gifford)

Since none of my friends were any more like Chip than I was, I had a difficult time believing that somebody like Chip could really exist. Even at twelve or thirteen years old it seemed too fantastic to me—especially since the still-reigning conception of Chicago boyhood was James T. Farrell's *Studs Lonigan* (which I was also reading in those days)—but I still read each new Hilton story as it appeared. I was actually kind of glad there was nobody in real life—*my* life—like him. It somehow made the books more exciting, and at that point I had no great interest in reality any-way.

Years later I found the first three Chip Hilton books selling for forty cents each in a used bookshop in New Orleans. I bought them and reread the first, *Touchdown Pass*. Since it had been written in 1948 some of the football information was outdated, rules had changed, and certain strategies and formations were no longer employed, but the descriptions of the games still rang true, and though Chip was certainly as premier a do-gooder and as invincible an athlete as I remembered, I was astonished to discover just how right it all felt. There were good guys and bad guys and in-between guys, and though the story was a rather obvious morality lesson, it all seemed sensible without being overly righteous or hopelessly corny. I couldn't help thinking that if Somerset Maugham had written American boys' sports stories they would have been something on the order of the Chip Hilton books.

In *Touchdown Pass*, Chip manages to help a friend's father find a job and get it back after he's lost it unfairly, captain and quarterback his high school team to the state championship de-spite a broken leg, and keep the peace among warring teammates. All of this is accomplished while Chip holds down a part-time job as a storeroom clerk each evening and is an outstanding student during the day. Pretty Jack Armstrong-ish to be sure, but Clair Bee made Chip a bit different, he made him moody and often mistaken and even vain. That Chip was always able to overcome these lapses in character was certainly unreal, and rarely was a girl mentioned, but at least there was something real about him.

I imagine that I must have learned something from reading

those books, and that I'm probably still operating according to some of those same principles and under those same delusions. What makes it possible to believe in something you know is impossible and to act as if it were not only possible but true? Maybe that's the only way anybody can ever really believe in anything.

TWENTY-SEVEN

Both Big Steve and I had pretty good Little League and Pony League careers. The best team either of us ever played on was my Royal Awning Liberty League team (thirteen to fifteen years old), which won 18 games in a row for the River Park championship in 1960. I was the youngest player on that team and didn't start until the third game of the season, even though I'd been an All-Star Little League third baseman the previous year. When I did get in, it was as an outfielder, and by the fifth game of the 20-game season I was the regular left fielder. That year I batted a league-leading—by 200 points!—.713.

In contrast to my previous season in Little League, where I'd been a long-ball hitter, in Liberty League I was a singles and doubles man, my longest hit of the year being a lone triple. I was always on base, however, stole about thirty times, and because we had so many powerful, good hitters behind me (I batted second in the order), I must have also led the league in runs scored. It was the single best season I ever had, including Little League, Pony League, high school, and college.

But the most outstanding game of my career was the final game of my last year in the River Park Little League play-offs. Our team had finished the regular season with a mediocre .500 record, and we were up against a team only slightly better than we were. They had one excellent pitcher who didn't allow a run against us that day, but our pitcher, an eleven-year-old named Larry, pitched a no-hitter against them and lost!

Big Steve was the official scorer for that game, his team having already been eliminated from the play-offs, and he needled me all through the game about my not being able to get a hit. I didn't do well, striking out twice and grounding out once to third, but nobody else was getting much either.

It was during this game that I really saw how crazed parents could get. Tony Kaufmann, the Cardinal scout who had found me playing baseball in the alley a few years before, warned me about the fans: "Don't listen to 'em," he said. "They're devils—one day you're a prince and the next they'd like to cut your throat. And all because you maybe muffed a grounder would have hit them between the eyes if they'd had the nerve to try for it." I'd always thought Tony had been talking about major league game spectators, but I was wrong.

When I came to bat for the second time in that Little League play-off game, the mother and father of my friend Mark Heath, at whose house I'd been playing two days before—Mark was in right field for the other team—began screaming and cursing at me from behind the backstop, telling me what a bum and a jerk I was. I really couldn't believe that it was Heath's parents saying such incredible things, especially to a twelve-year-old, so I stepped back out of the batter's box and stared at them. I tried to heed Tony's warning and ignore them, but they were so close and so loud that it was impossible. They continued ranting and cheered like crazy when I tapped out weakly to the third baseman. I never could bring myself to go over to Mark Heath's house after that.

Going into the top half of the last inning, Larry, our pitcher, still hadn't allowed the hint of a hit. Their first batter, however, hit a genuine shot to my left which I dived for, prevented from going through to the outfield, picked up, got to my feet, and threw to first base. The runner beat my throw by a step and Steve scored it as an error on me. While I was rooting for Larry to pitch a no-hitter, this judgment seemed to be stretching it a little; I didn't deserve an error on that play and I was angry about Big Steve's assessment.

The really unfortunate part of the situation was that after

stealing second base and going to third on a fly ball the runner scored on a fielder's choice. The batter hit a ground ball to second and our second baseman fired the ball home. The runner slid in under the tag and was called safe by Fat Wally, the worst umpire in the league. Fat Wally literally could not see over his enormous gut.

After Wally called the runner safe, I exploded. I started yelling at him and threw my glove, which bounced off his face mask. Fat Wally then threw me out of the game. Our coach came running over and begged Wally to leave me in. I was the only third baseman on the team, he said, I'd lost my temper but I'd be all right, I wouldn't do it again, something like that. I don't know what all the coach said, but Wally agreed to let me remain in the game so long as I didn't open my mouth. I was due up in the last half of the inning and the coach knew I had the best chance of anyone on our team to hit one out.

When we came in from the field Big Steve taunted me about the error and I turned and attacked him. It was a good thing my teammates got me away before he killed me. As it was he was so surprised by my reaction that he just backed off and looked at me with a confused expression. Anyway, after our first batter struck out, I calmed down enough to get up to the plate, where I went down swinging on three pitches. The next batter, however, walked, as did the next, and the next. Their pitcher had suddenly gotten very wild, a common occurrence in Little League games, and with our pitcher, Larry, coming up, we had a good chance to tie or win.

The count on Larry went to 3 and 2 and the place was going crazy. All of us were standing up, hanging on the next pitch. Their pitcher went into a full windup and threw the ball as hard as he could. It came in fast, but low, so low, in fact, that it hit about two feet in front of the plate and bounced into the catcher's mitt at about Larry's knee level. Larry dropped his bat and began his trot to first base. Our bench was cheering and the runner came home from third to tie the game.

But all of a sudden the other team was jumping up and down on each other and yelling that they'd won. Fat Wally had called the last pitch a strike! He hadn't seen it bounce in and thought that when it passed Larry at the knees it had come in on the fly. It was unbelievable! Our entire team screamed at him. Our coach threw his hat, which hit Wally on the mask, just as my glove had. Wally tried to throw him out of the game, only he couldn't: due to his horrendous call, it was already over.

Big Steve sat on the bench and laughed. I went over and sat down next to him and laughed too. We couldn't even see Fat Wally at the plate, he was so surrounded by coaches and players and parents. Mark Heath's mother was standing on the pitcher's mound with Mark, brushing dirt off his pants. I told Steve I was sorry for attacking him and he said to forget it. We shook hands, I changed into my street shoes, and we walked home together like we always did.

TWENTY-EIGHT

There are moments in a ballplayer's life, whether in fact or fiction, upon which his entire career might depend. *Never Come Back*, a novel by Frank O'Rourke, was a baseball story that for the first time showed me there was more to baseball players than baseball. I'd heard about the girl who'd shot Eddie Waitkus in a Philadelphia hotel room, and the girl who'd shot Cub shortstop Billy Jurges in the hand, but those were legendary incidents that apparently needed no explanation. Nobody offered me one when I asked about them, and since I was only about eleven or twelve when I read O'Rourke's book, baseball was really all I wanted to think about.

Coming across O'Rourke's story about a washed-up out-fielder named Hub Maloski, who's offered a chance to make some big dough by fixing a big game, was a surprise to me. The fix angle wasn't such a surprise. I'd read about the Black Sox scandal by then, and living in Chicago, crookedness seemed the natural way of life; my dad and most of my friends' fathers were hooked up to the rackets in one form or another, so that didn't mean much. It was that the bribe offer was presented by Hub's ex-wife, a no-good dame who, knowing Hub was down on his luck, came to see him wearing a mink stole.

The book began in a bar, the long shadow of the barroom, where men could lose themselves or be easily lost, something like that. I didn't understand drinking then, or why men drank, but I had an intuitive understanding about a blonde in a mink coming to bribe Hub.

Don Landrum (Courtesy of George Brace)

The point was that the veteran Hub had fought his way back to one final good season, he was too old to play regularly anymore, and his team was now either in the Series or playing for the pennant. He'd be in a position at least to affect the score, but of course he didn't do it. I don't remember now whether or not his team won or lost the game, but Hub held onto his honor.

That's how it was in those books—Duane Decker's Blue Sox series, Jackson Scholz's *Perfect Game*, Clair Bee's Chip Hilton, John Tunis's *The Kid from Tompkinsville*—the '30s tradition, men walked with hands in their pockets, whistling, as Jack Kerouac fondly recalled; and they held on to their honor, no matter what, or else consigned themselves to the gutter and, ultimately, the devil.

Looking through *The Baseball Encyclopedia* one day, I came across the unusual name of Royce Lint. Royce James Lint pitched in 30 games for the St. Louis Cardinals in 1954. He was born in Birmingham, Alabama, on New Year's Day in 1921, so he had been a thirty-three-year-old rookie pitcher. He was a lean (six-one, 165 pounds) left-hander, threw and batted lefty. Not much of a hitter, he went 1 for 10 in his one season, but then not many pitchers hit well.

Royce started 4 games. His record on the season was 2 wins and 3 losses, all but one of those decisions coming in relief. The lone decision as a starter was a shutout victory. In one game he pitched the full nine innings and didn't allow a run. Royce pitched only 18 1/3 innings as a starter, so in 3 games he pitched a total of 9 1/3 innings, lasting an average of only 3 or so a game. But in that one start, incredibly, he went the distance and blanked the other team.

I don't imagine Royce was much of a traveler, except when he went from team to team in the minor leagues. I like to think that Royce Lint went back to Birmingham each fall, that after he stopped playing, whenever he watched the Game of the Week on television or listened to an Atlanta Braves or—before the Braves moved to Georgia—St. Louis game, he remembered his shutout, his one outstanding moment that was an irrevocable entry in the record book. That may have made it not matter that he worked on an assembly line or not at all. His achievement was permanent and worthy of envy by every boy who ever dreamed of playing in the major leagues.

Royce and Hub and Al Gionfriddo, who made that amazing one-handed leaping catch of DiMaggio's drive practically into the seats in the 1947 Series and was back in the minors the next season, had something to cherish, an inviolable, untouchable, pristine story-bookish act captured forever, not only in memory or imagination but in print, be it *The Baseball Encyclopedia* or *Never Come Back*. Anyone, as Casey Stengel would say, could look it up and see what it was, when it was and always will be, ex-wives in minks notwithstanding.

TWENTY-NINE

The National League did indeed expand in 1962, and gave the half-lie to the previous season's joke that with expansion the Cubs would finish eighth and not be in the cellar. They finished an embarrassing ninth, 5 games behind the neophyte Houston Colt .45s; only the immediately infamous New York Metropolitans, managed by Yankee castoff Casey Stengel, kept the Cubs from finishing dead last.

The year 1962 was the one Ernie Banks made the shift to first base so that Andre Rodgers, a former Cricket player, could take over at short, a decision one might credit to any one or all three of the Cub coaches that season. The revolving-door managerial system remained in effect (and equally ineffectual) with El Tappe (4 and 16), Lou Klein (12 and 18), and Charlie Metro (43 and 69) sharing the blame. George Altman continued to wield a big bat, hitting .318 and 22 home runs; Billy Williams improved his average by 20 points to .298, driving in 91 runs to boot; Lou Brock became a regular and hit .263, including a 485-foot-plus home run in the Polo Grounds against the Mets.

For the second year in a row the Cubs came up with the National League rookie of the year, second baseman Ken Hubbs, a better-than-average hitter with remarkable range and poise in the field. He promised to be the Cub second-sacker of the forseeable future; it was the unforseeable part, however, that came to bear in Hubbs's case. Banks had another remarkable season at the plate, knocking 37 homers and batting in 104 runs, improving his

RBI total over 1961 by 24. Ernie's accomplishment can be further appreciated when one considers that the Cubs finished two places below their position the previous season and the team runs total, even though 8 games had been added to the schedule to accommodate the expansion clubs, *dropped* by 57! Ron Santo hit only .227, and Dick Bertell, the regular catcher much of the campaign, though he averaged .302, batted in an anemic 18 runs.

Bob Buhl, Dick Ellsworth, Don Cardwell, Glen Hobbie, Bob Anderson, rookie Cal Koonce, and the others on the pitching staff combined for a team ERA of 4.54, tying the Mets for fewest shutouts with 4. Their total of 29 complete games was lowest in the league by far. Only Don Elston, coming in from the bullpen earlier and earlier, game after game, had a decent season.

For a couple of reasons, though, 1962 was a banner year at Wrigley Field for me and Big Steve. One big event was the second All-Star game (the leagues played two each season from 1958 to 1962) on July 30. Steve and I were determined to have our regular bleacher seats for the game and so joined an already considerable bleachers box office queue at four o'clock the morning of the game. Fans had set up card tables, playing by lantern light; some were wrapped up in sleeping bags; others were crouched down against the wall passing wine or whiskey bottles. The ticket sale began about ten and Steve and I managed to secure our places in right-center field.

Oddly enough, the American League won that game, 9 to 4, in something less than a nail-biter. During batting practice Rocky Colavito, who was running in the outfield, tossed several balls up into the bleachers, which turned out to be the highlight of the day. Colavito, the great Cleveland and Detroit slugger, reinforced his popularity later when he socked a 3-run homer into the left-field seats.

Another highlight involved Big Steve's friend Cliff, who worked as a vendor in the bleachers. Cliff was always getting into fights and one day he attacked a customer with his hot dog tray strung around his neck. Cliff dived into a row of fans in an effort to strangle his adversary, spraying hot dogs, hot water, and buns on whoever happened to be in the way.

The outstanding occurrence of the 1962 season, however, was the Cubs' acquisition, a third of the way into that disastrous campaign, of journeyman outfielder Don Landrum from St. Louis. Landrum, a twenty-six-year-old left-handed hitter of no particular renown, had never really been given much of an opportunity to display his talents, whatever they might be, until he came to the Cubs. Neither the Phillies nor the Cards, the two teams he'd spent time with prior to his arrival in Chicago, had played him with any regularity despite his fairly impressive minor league record, and he was expected to battle Lou Brock for the center-field job.

What happened was that, for whatever reason, Big Steve, who by this time had established himself absolutely as the number one Bleacher Bum bigmouth, decided to concentrate all of his energy on giving Landrum the hardest time of his major league life. Steve was merciless in his verbal assault on poor Donnie, calling him a bum at every opportunity, regardless of whether or not Landrum had done anything to elicit such abuse. Steve was extremely loud, occasionally witty, and had developed quite a following of bleacher denizens. Once Steve started to pick up a chorus of supporters Landrum didn't stand a chance. For his part, Landrum was mystified by the whole thing. While not a great player, he wasn't terrible, either. He batted .286 that year and didn't do badly in the field, but Big Steve was relentless in his somewhat terrifying obsession. He organized a "Landrum Is a Bum Sign Day," when twenty or thirty fans in the right-center-field bleachers brought homemade placards denigrating Donnie in a variety of verbiage.

If at first Landrum was mystified, his attitude toward Big Steve soon became, not unpredictably, hostile, and he spent a considerable amount of his outfield service shouting back at the stands. This display of emotion, of course, only served to aggravate the situation, inspiring Steve and his legion of Landrum-baiters to new forms of public outrage. It took Landrum until the following season before he figured out how to quell the beast Big Steve had become. He came over and asked Steve why he was being so cruel, to which Steve had no real answer. Landrum continued to speak calmly to Steve before and during the ensuing games, and soon they were on a first-name basis. Eventually Landrum began giving Big Steve gifts: baseballs, bats, even a perfectly worked-in, oil-blackened glove. Steve treasured the glove and used it at every opportunity until it was stolen a couple of years later. He and Don Landrum became buddies, exchanging family news, and Steve started the Don Landrum Fan Club.

The ironic thing was that after Steve and Landrum made peace Landrum's performance declined considerably. His .286 season was followed by a .242 in 1963, an 0 for 11 disaster in '64 (he was injured that year), and a .226 in '65. Finally the Cubs gave up on Donnie and sent him to San Francisco, where he batted a pathetic .186. That was his last attempt at being a major league ballplayer, and the last we heard, in 1967, was that Landrum was selling cars somewhere in northern California.

Don Landrum's departure from Chicago was a real blow to Big Steve; he sincerely missed him. I believe that by being kind Landrum had taught Big Steve a bit of a lesson—at least I never saw Steve get quite as exercised in his ballpark abuse after the Landrum Affair.

THIRTY

During the off-seasons I'd spend a considerable amount of time playing All-Star Baseball, a Cadaco-Ellis board game with player cards that fit around spinners which pointed to numbers on the cards, dictating the action. Seven was a single, 5 a triple, 2 a fly ball, 11 a double, 1 a home run, and so forth. I spent hours absorbed in this game. Each card represented an individual player, and I made up an All-Star All-Star team that practically never lost. My biggest star was Gus Zernial, the old Philadelphia and White Sox outfielder, whose card had the widest home run area. He blasted 100 homers one season for me, and drove in more than 200 runs. I treasured Zernial's card, refusing dozens of times to trade or sell it to other All-Star Baseball Game aficionados, using it over and over until it was gray, tattered, and limp. Only the Ernie Banks and Ted Williams cards came close to being as valuable as Zernial, though among my personal favorites were Minnie Minoso, Chico Carrasquel (of course), and Ed Mathews, who one year almost eclipsed Gus with 98 home runs. My mother thought I spent entirely too much time playing this game, even though I explained that by keeping such a volume of statistics as I did I was improving my arithmetical acumen. She thought it was a waste of time, and there really was no way I could express to her the magic

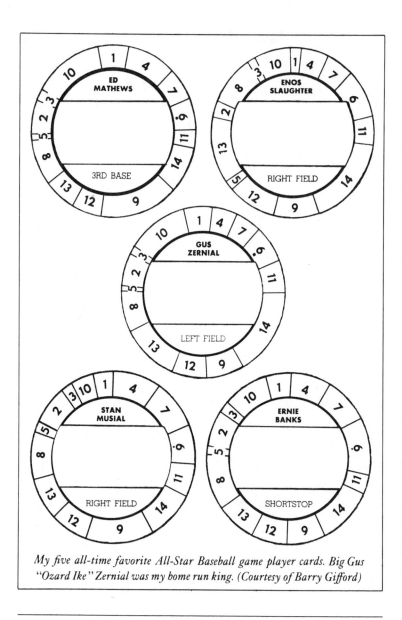

My five all-time favorite All-Star Baseball game player cards. Big Gus "Ozard Ike" Zernial was my home run king. (Courtesy of Barry Gifford)

and beauty inherent in a cardboard circle labeled Gus Zernial.*

But in the early winter of 1962–63 the outdoor activity was football, not baseball, though there was considerable speculation regarding a rise in Cub fortunes with the recent acquisition of pitchers Larry Jackson and Lindy McDaniel from St. Louis. Jackson had always been a steady 15-, 16-, or 18-game winner, and McDaniel had been an outstanding reliever. This particular afternoon the field at GB was mud and slush and there were mounds of dirty snow along the sidelines. Big Steve was limping around on crutches, having just gotten out of the hospital after a knee operation, making bets on the Cubs' not finishing out of the second division in the coming season. Since he couldn't play he was acting as our team's coach.

I was playing cornerback on defense, halfback on offense, for the GB All-Stars against the St. Tim's Rejects. The team name "GB All-Stars"—GB stood for Green Briar Park, of course—was agreed upon by the players as a compromise moniker. Dozens of names were proposed. My own favorite—nominated by our tackle Billy "the Demon" Demonzakis—was the Union Laguna White Devils, inspired by the team of the same name in the Mexican Professional Baseball League. Billy had gotten it out of *The Sporting News*. To Billy's and my dismay, even though we agreed to modify the name to the *Green Briar* White Devils, it was voted down by a large margin.

The Rejects—kids who'd been thrown out of St. Timothy's school—were a better team than we were, held regular practices,

---

*Not long after I wrote this paragraph, my mother sent me my old All-Star Baseball game. On January 9, 1981, I played a game against a friend who was using a 1979 set of player discs. He had once owned his own version of the game, in the late '40s in the Bronx, and throughout our contest I kept telling him how valuable and magical Gus Zernial's card had always been to me, how Gus had always come through in the clutch. As fate decreed it, we went into the bottom of the 10th inning tied up 6 to 6, with Zernial coming to bat. I hadn't played this game for twenty years but I had complete faith in the raggedy cardboard Gus, who promptly justified his mythological status as the spinner head, at the conclusion of its cycle, pointed directly to the number one at the top of Zernial's card, signifying a home run, winning the game.

and had played together longer; but we were rougher and unpredictable and had beaten everyone else in the club league, which consisted of five teams representing neighborhood gangs. Each team played the others twice, making an eight-game season, this game marking the halfway point.

Heavy Ed Duda, the Rejects' center Bob Duda's older brother, who was a neighborhood football legend, having scored seven touchdowns in the club league championship game four years before, was one of the officials. The other was another local legend, Little Lennie Lassiter, older brother of our left end Roger Raymond's girl friend Terry, who'd been an All-City high school halfback three years in a row. Lassiter wore black, low-cut moccasins in all weathers, even now in the slop, somehow never slipping, running faster than any of us to stay on top of the play. The officials were respected and agreed upon by both teams so there would be no arguments.

The first half was one slip after another—neither team could get going in the mud, and nobody scored. The closest call came when Johnny MacGowan, the Rejects' fastest back, who wore a white helmet with a black feather fixed sticking up out of one of the air holes, picked up a fumble by our fullback, Fireworks Kammeyer, and tightroped twenty-nine yards down the sideline to our five before Roger Raymond muscled him out of bounds. I intercepted MacGowan's pass into the end zone on the next play, and that ended the threat.

The game was eight-man tackle—two ends, two tackles, center, and three shotgun backs—with little or no equipment. Nobody under fourteen or over eighteen was allowed to play. There were rarely any injuries, the worst I'd ever seen being the time Morris Mankowitz, the Wreckers' four-foot eleven-inch fullback, was fallen on while trying to recover a fumble by the Night Roamers' fifteen-year-old, 290-pound tackle Sid "the Bronc" Bronkowski, and broke his collarbone. Other than that there were occasional broken ribs and sprained wrists and ankles. Each club kept a supply of Popsicle sticks and a roll of adhesive tape to set jammed and busted fingers on the spot. Some players wore mouthpieces to protect their teeth, but if you did that it was

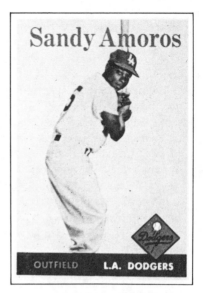

Andy Pafko

(Courtesy of Barry Gifford)

difficult to shout directions or warnings, so it was a rule on our team that nobody could use one.

The second half was as sloppy as the first, only more desperate. Neither team wanted a tie and there were more long passes and wide power sweeps. Johnny MacGowan made two long runs but they couldn't score. Just when it looked like they'd make it somebody would slip or fumble, and the same thing happened to us. Everyone was wet and caked with mud, and with five minutes to go Fireworks Kammeyer got upset about something and punched one of the Rejects. Beef Bufante, our center, jumped the Reject Kammeyer had punched, and before it was over, Ed Duda and Lennie Lassiter had to kick in a couple of heads. Both the Beef and Fireworks were thrown out of the game. The Reject they'd worked over had a broken nose but wanted to play and stayed in.

The Rejects got down to our twenty on a long pass and on the next play Johnny MacGowan went wide around the left side led by Giant Jack Mooney. Mooney came up on me and tried a roll block, but I delayed a fraction of a second, hurdled him, and knocked MacGowan down for a seven-yard loss, smashing his feather in the process. Mooney clapped me on the back on his way back to the huddle. I glared at him and he grinned. Mooney was about six-two or -three and easily the toughest kid on the St. Tim's team. I felt pretty good having light-stepped him, but he was a great blocker and I hoped they'd go the other way on the next play.

They came straight at me again. I could see MacGowan with the ball, half a feather sticking cockily out of his now brown helmet, laying back, waiting for Mooney to clear the way. Mooney went into another roll and I held up the way I had before, but this time he caught my left foot and steamrolled right over me, knocking me flat on my back and smothering me with his body. Out of the corner of my eye I caught MacGowan's quick cut back inside and I reached frantically with my left hand for his flashing leg. He was by me and gone and the Rejects had six points. They kicked the extra point and the score stayed at 7–zip until the last ten seconds of the game.

On the last play of the final series our quarterback, Sid Guglielmi, for the first time in his life emulating his cousin Ralph, threw a perfect fly pattern pass to Danny Dewey, our fastest end, that went for a touchdown. We had a chance to tie it and I looked to the sidelines for Harmon Horowitz, our kicker. The only time Harmon ever got into the game was on extra point tries.

Harmon replaced Dewey and then Big Steve, without his crutches, limped onto the field and told Sid to get off. I couldn't believe it, but Steve, as coach, was putting himself in to hold the ball for the point try. It seemed crazy to me, Steve could get his leg permanently crushed, and I told him so, but he just said to shut up and block.

The snap came back to Big Steve, he placed the ball down, but just as Harmon's foot came up to boot it Steve snatched it away, got to his feet, and started limping around like a wounded buffalo. He was going to try to pass the ball for the two points that would win the game, but he couldn't find a receiver. Of course nobody on our team had any idea that Steve would put himself into the game, let alone run around with a broken knee trying to throw a pass, and there was nobody in the end zone.

Finally, out of desperation, Steve tossed the ball underhanded to me, crumpled to the ground, and covered his head with his arms. I was right in front of him trying to block, and just as I caught the ball (by reflex—if I'd had a second to think I would have dropped it) Giant Jack Mooney cut me down. The game was over and Mooney offered me his hand, but I just rolled over and rested my head in the mud. The cold ground felt good and anyway there was no reason to get up.

THIRTY-ONE

A popular summer sport in the neighborhood was whiffle ball, which we played at the end of the alley behind my house, where I'd met Tony Kaufmann, the St. Louis Cardinal scout. For a backstop we used the outside rear wall of the old red Crackerbox Grill, a tiny cottage just down the alley from Beebs and Glen's Tavern. On summer nights we'd play until after it got dark. The rules were identical to those for fast ball pitching, the only difference in the game being the ball itself (whiffle balls are white plastic with holes in them so as to make them move more radically, like a knuckle ball) and the distance between pitcher and batter, which was greatly reduced. The old lady who ran the Crackerbox never complained, and in fact was always glad to see us and say a few words whenever she came out back to dump the garbage.

On dark winter afternoons I liked to sit inside the Crackerbox on one of the wobbly stools, sipping a hot chocolate, and listen to the neighborhood janitors gossip and complain in Swedish. The old lady fry cook could whip up a couple of eggs, toast, bacon, oatmeal, all at the same time she was handling and handing over orders for three, four more customers just whisked in the door.

Not only was the little wooden Crackerbox Grill cheap but good. It was even exciting, what with fugitive types speaking in whispers. Once I overheard two of them talking over plans to rob a bank, or thought I did. I couldn't believe it, and when I realized

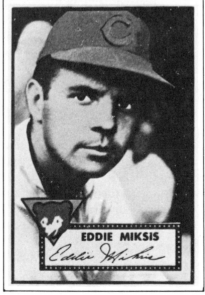

107

they probably weren't fooling I looked around and they were gone. One, perhaps both, were Indians, probably hauled from Dakota to Chicago for "relocation," with no job prospects but steel work, iron work, then layoff. Not unlikely bank robbers.

I was always impressed by the patience of the place, and fascinated by the lonely booze-beat bums who'd loiter over a dime coffee for two or more hours and then shove a nickel across the counter.

"Coffee's a dime," the old lady'd say, looking at the red-nosed derelict in his mothy, ragged St. Vincent DePaul oversized overcoat slept in that winter and last.

"Only *got* a nickel," the deep-voiced but calm bum's answer, one eye at the price board over the grill, the other not-focused directly at the cook.

"Okay," was her inevitable reply. "And button up that coat," she'd shout at him, "it's windy out there."

Without a further word the yellow-white-haired hobo, hair now graying and dirty like cloudy but sun-blotched and streaked southwest Texas skies, would rise, seeming to tower in the tiny hovel diner, and stumble out. The wind would beat back the door with a slam, and the old guy would stand a minute in the blow, leaning, deciding finally which way to go, which alleys to walk until the mealtime mission opened.

The cook would cluck her tongue, lick her fuzzy upper lip, spin eggs off the grill with expert timing to a plate, picking up rolls or coffee or milk (or all) on the way, and set it before the customer without so much as a slight clack of plate on the Formica countertop.

A few days after I'd overheard the two Indians whispering about blowing a bank two blue-faced detectives stopped in the Crackerbox. I figured they were taking a break from tracking down the robbers, glad to be in out of the snow, hats still on.

"Afternoon, ma'am."

"Hello, boys. Two coffees?"

The janitor at the end of the counter finished up and walked out without a look at them. He doesn't like cops, either, I thought —especially detectives.

The last time I went in there, not long before I graduated from high school, the old lady said she was on her way to Nevada at the end of that week, just before Christmas. The Crackerbox was closing down.

"Why Nevada?" I asked.

"That's where my daughter lives," she said. "I been here twenty-five years."

Years later I heard someone say that the most likely murderers are short-order cooks, because of the pressure they're under all day. I thought immediately of the woman at the Crackerbox and how that didn't apply to her, not that sturdy lady with her brown wad of bun hair I'd never seen again. It's the plainclothes cops' consciences that must suffer Christmases, I thought; and the paranoid, dark-eyed Indian bandits, likely-to-backfire-if-fired pawnshop Saturday night specials in their leather jacket pockets.

After the Crackerbox closed we still used it for our whiffle ball field. It never reopened but stood abandoned for years, finally being torn down a few years after I'd gone away. I never did find out where it was the janitors hung out after the place shut down.

THIRTY-TWO

Nineteen sixty-three was the Year of the Pitcher, especially in the National League, where Sandy Koufax of the Dodgers and Juan Marichal of the Giants each won 25 games, while Warren Spahn of Milwaukee (at the age of forty-two) and Jim Maloney of Cincinnati won 23 each and—surprise!—Dick Ellsworth of the Cubs won 22, including four shutouts. Not only that, but the lanky southpaw lost only 10 and compiled a brilliant 2.11 ERA. It was to be Ellsworth's best season in the majors by far. He never again finished with even a break-even won-lost record in the National League; he would, however, make a one-season comeback in 1968 with the Boston Red Sox, winning 16 games.

Lindy McDaniel had a sterling year in relief for the Cubs, finishing 13 and 7, with 22 saves and a 2.86 ERA. Larry Jackson pitched in tough all season, compiling a 2.55 ERA, winning 14 games but dropping 18. It was a competitive staff. The starting rotation of Ellsworth, Jackson, Buhl, and Hobbie (who seemed somewhat rehabilitated) was good enough to keep the Cubs above .500 for the season, winding up 82 and 80, the team's best won-lost mark since its 77 wins and 77 losses under Phil Cavarretta in 1952.

Many fans credited the new—and only—head coach, Bob Kennedy, for the resurgence. The one thing everybody did agree on was that the rotating coach system had been a failure. Despite the Cubs' first plus season in eighteen years, they still finished in the second division, a distant seventh ahead of only Pittsburgh, Houston, and the Mets. (Big Steve won his bets.)

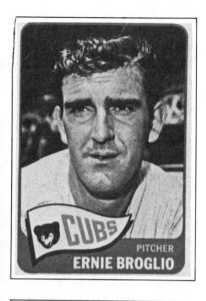

(Courtesy of Barry Gifford)

Oddly enough, considering their improved record, only two Cubs had good seasons at the plate: Ron Santo, who came back to hit .297 with 25 home runs and 99 RBI; and Billy Williams, at .286, 25, and 95. Banks slumped badly to .227, with only 18 round-trippers and 64 RBI; Ken Hubbs, 1962's rookie of the year, batted .235; and the Bahamas' own Andre Rodgers, while leading the National League's shortstops in errors with 35, patty-caked a weak .229.

Newcomer Ellis Burton, who replaced George Altman in centerfield, hit .230; Lou Brock, who showed flashes of brilliance both at bat and in the field while copping 24 bases, wound up with a .258 average; and catcher Dick Bertell's bat mark dipped 69 points to .233. Don Landrum, Big Steve's pal, hit .242. It was hardly a sparkling bunch of sticks. Nevertheless, Cub fans were encouraged by the team's improved record.

If they had examined the statistics closely, however, they would have noticed that the Cubs' 82 wins were accomplished largely at the expense of the lowly expansion clubs. Houston lost 96 games and New York 111. Bob Kennedy boasted that the Cubs were on the move, and he was correct. Unfortunately, as Big Steve and I predicted, they were once again moving in the wrong direction.

THIRTY-THREE

Nineteen sixty-four was the last year I lived in Chicago and, therefore, was the last season I was able to attend Cub games on a regular basis. It was the first season Ron Santo hit .300, a feat he would accomplish twice more in his career; it was also the year Billy Williams first batted better than .300, a figure he would surpass five times in his baseball lifetime. During 1964 I first got an inkling that the Cincinnati second baseman, Pete Rose, then in his second season and averaging in the .260s, just might turn out to be more than an average ballplayer. It was also the last year of the great New York Yankee dynasty established by Casey Stengel, continued under the leadership of Ralph Houk, and now come to rest in first place in the American League regardless of the manager, who happened to be, of all people, Yogi Berra. ("Ninety percent of the game is talent," said the Yog, "the other half is mental.") But the most remarkable and distressing fact of the 1964 campaign was the taking of the National League pennant and subsequent victory over the Yankees in the World Series by the St. Louis Cardinals, who were led to the championship of major league baseball by Louis Clark Brock.

In an early-season effort to bolster the pitching staff, the Cub management traded, as the principal in a multi-player deal, out-fielder Lou Brock, who, after 52 games, was batting .251, to St. Louis for, among other players, right-handed hurler Ernie Broglio, who, to that point in the season, had compiled a 3 and 5 won-lost record. On the face of it the Cubs had not made a bad deal. In years to come it would, to my mind, be equalled in lopsided results only by the San Francisco Giant trade of George Foster to Cincinnati for Frank Duffy and Vern Geishart. To be sure, there have been other deals the outcome of which turned out to be decidedly one-sided, but the one I can never expunge from memory is the Brock-Broglio swap.

Ernie Broglio's won-lost record from 1959 to 1963 was 67 and 50. He was twenty-eight years old when the Cubs obtained him. In Brock's two full seasons with the Cubs he had batted .263 and .258. He was twenty-four years old when they let him go. Broglio finished the '64 season for the Cubs 4 and 7 with a 4.04 ERA. Lou Brock batted .348 for St. Louis that year and wound up the regular season with 43 stolen bases. He hit .300 in the World Series, in which he did not steal a base. He went on, however, to swipe 14 bases in two subsequent World Series, and to accumulate more than 900 stolen bases in his 19 major league seasons, more than any other player, ever. His 933rd theft broke Sliding Billy Hamilton's pre-modern-era record; Ty Cobb, before Brock considered the greatest base stealer in modern baseball history, was left in the dust at 892. On his way to stealing all those bases, in the service of accomplishing the prerequisite, Brock, whom the Cubs saw fit to sacrifice for Mr. Broglio, hit safely better than 3,000 times, an achievement—as if his phenomenal stolen base total were in itself insufficient—that ensured him a place in baseball's Hall of Fame. Ernie Broglio's cumulative record for the Cubs from 1964 to 1966 (his last season in the majors—Brock played until 1980) was 6 wins, 17 losses.

I watched Brock play for St. Louis in the 1964 Series with mixed emotions. My consternation was at least partially due to the fact of my being resident at the University of Missouri. Everyone around me was rooting, of course, for the Cardinals, and I resented seeing Brock in a Redbird uniform. People were constantly referring to the Broglio trade, and my ears burned. What could I say? *I* hadn't made the deal. Silently, I rooted for the Yankees, keeping to myself my belief that Bob Gibson, Brock, Curt Flood, Bill White, and Kenny Boyer were too much for them. The Cardinals were hungrier and livelier; New York,

(Courtesy of Barry Gifford)

though powerful, looked just a bit dull, uninterested, and the Cards' edge gave them the seventh game and the Series. Lou Brock came of age suddenly and dramatically in 1964—to be precise, in June of that year, as soon as he left Chicago.

As for the Cubs, they finished eighth, 10 games below .500. Kenny Hubbs, the sparkplug second baseman, had died the previous February 14, Valentine's Day, in a small-plane crash over Provo, Utah, and there was a pall over the team all season. Santo, Williams (who hit 33 homers), and Banks all had good years with the bat, but nobody else could hit a lick, and only ex-Cardinal Larry Jackson had a good year on the hill, recording an incredible 24 victories, nearly a full third of the Cubs' wins. (Somebody joked that Jackson, too, was caught up in the Cardinals' pennant fever, and pretended he was still in a St. Louis uniform whenever he went to the mound.) Lew Burdette, the hero of the 1957 World Series for the Milwaukee Braves, joined the club, winning 9 and losing 9. Journeyman Len Gabrielson replaced Brock in the outfield and hit .246.

After the season, head coach Bob Kennedy said the Cubs needed to fill a few holes. (Being that this was Chicago, wags were prone to twist this assessment slightly, opining that what was really required were a few well-placed holes in the Cub front office.) Kennedy did not, however, commit himself as to whether or not the Cubs were still on the move. I was, though I had no idea, that summer of '64, that I would not witness the Cubs frolic again in Wrigley Field for fourteen seasons.

THIRTY-FOUR

By the time I got to college my enthusiasm for competitive athletics had waned considerably from what it once had been. My interests were shifting and expanding, and while sports was a way for me to survive the psychological—as well as physical—rigors of life in the old neighborhood, once I had departed that environment I was eager to take advantage of the freedom my leaving provided.

I played baseball at Missouri but my heart was not in the game. I became a pitcher, rather than the infielder I'd been scouted as, and relied heavily on finesse as opposed to the fastball my arm no longer seemed able to possess. (Too many games of Fastball!) My relationship with the coaches was not what it might have been—especially since I spent much of my time hanging out at the local coffeehouse among the very few "subversive" types on campus—but I got along fine with my teammates. A number of recent Tiger players had signed lucrative bonus contracts with major league teams—Missouri ("Mizzou," the students called it) had been very successful in the Big 8 conference under Coach Hi Simmons—and expectations of the same were prevalent among the squad's better prospects, the best of whom I thought was an outfielder named Gene Raymore. I corresponded with Gene for several years after I left the university—following my first, and last, year—but then, the times being as frantic as they were (for me, anyway), I stopped writing, and when I finally did write, after almost a decade, I received no reply.

Gene Raymore was a quiet kid from a small town in Oklahoma. I met him on the first day of baseball practice at the university, to which he'd come, he explained, to play ball and get a degree in physical education so that he could go back to the small town and be a high school baseball coach and gym instructor. Though he was a genuine major league prospect, had received offers of minor league contracts following graduation from high school, and would subsequently receive several more such opportunities during his college career, Gene never really considered himself big league material. He was a small-town boy (though not the Chip Hilton type) and was serious when he said he had no intention of taking up life in the big city, any city.

He joined a relatively low-profile fraternity and spent his nights watching television and drinking beer. He wasn't big, about five-nine, 155 pounds, wore glasses, was left-handed. He was a steady, solid ballplayer, hit to all fields. He could play left or right field—didn't have the speed for center—and the coaches liked him. Most of the other boys in the fraternity liked him, too. They left him alone when they saw that he liked to keep to himself. An athlete was good to have in the house, lent it prestige, so they rarely bothered him about participating in campus events.

One night, late, after midnight, during his junior year, Gene heard a scream from in back of the fraternity house. He was watching TV and figured it was one of the guys coming in drunk, so he ignored it. The second scream he did not ignore since he recognized it as a female scream. He dropped his beer on the couch and dashed out the rear door. He smelled something burning, ran around to the side parking lot, and saw Jim Morris, one of his fraternity brothers, shielding his eyes from the blinding glare of a flaming mattress.

"I couldn't stop her!" Morris yelled.

There was a body in the middle of the flames. Gene grabbed one end of the mattress and began dragging it around the parking lot, turning it from side to side and then over, tumbling the body onto the gravel. The girl's body was badly charred—the smell was terrible. Gene ran into the house and called the Fire Department. When he hung up he saw that the hair on his hands and arms had been burned off, as were his eyebrows and part of his scalp.

The girl had had too much to drink, Jim Morris explained, and had been smoking dope. She'd become depressed about the war, how none of the marches did enough good. Only the Buddhist monks and nuns who had immolated themselves seemed to attract any serious attention, she'd said. Morris had watched while she poured gasoline on the mattress he'd dragged up from the basement. He hadn't really thought she would go through with it and then suddenly she sat down on the mattress and lit a match. There was nothing he could do, Morris said.

The next year Gene Raymore graduated from Missouri, rejected a modest offer from the Pittsburgh organization and a better than modest offer from the Mets, and went back to Oklahoma, where he got a job at his hometown high school as a P.E. instructor and baseball and junior varsity basketball coach. The Army didn't want him because of a bad knee. He would have gone to Vietnam if he had had to, he wrote me, but he had not, and in a few more years the war was over.

THIRTY-FIVE

I followed the doings of the 1965 season as best I could in the Paris edition of the *New York Times*. I was living in London and Wrigley Field seemed a million light-years away. Via the *Times*'s one-page sports section I learned of Cincinnati pitcher Jim Maloney's second no-hitter of the season, versus the Cubs, on August 9; and of Sandy Koufax's perfect game, exactly one month later, also against the Cubs.

Head coach Bob Kennedy must have been consulting the *I Ching* for directions regarding his club, which had continued to slide since their above .500 mark of two years before. Whatever, nothing he did could prevent the Cubs from finishing in eighth place again, but to his undoubted relief, he wasn't around to witness that season's denouement in person. The Cub management, insisting that the rotating coach system was actually still in effect, replaced Kennedy 56 games into the season with one of the original rotaters, Lou Klein. Kennedy departed with the team 8 games on the distaff side of .500, and by the time Klein was through they were 18 below.

However, the new keystone combination of Glenn Beckert at second and Don Kessinger at shortstop debuted in '65. They were to anchor the Cubs at their positions for years to come, playing together through 1973; that would have been hard to predict that first season, Beckert batting only .239 and Kessinger .201 while leading the National League in errors with 28. Banks had a remarkable year, driving in 106 runs and belting 28 home runs. Santo became the consummate third baseman, a legitimate All-Star, and hit .285, with 33 homers and 101 RBI.

Billy Williams was again the only outfielder worth his pay, and he was that and then some, taking his place among the top sluggers in the league with 34 homers, 108 RBI, and a .315 average. None of the other pasture performers—Doug Clemens, Don Landrum (the same), and Jimmy Stewart—could hit better than .226. Bob Buhl was the only starting pitcher to finish with a winning record (13 and 11); and if it hadn't been for submarine-ball pitcher Ted Abernathy's 31 saves and 2.57 ERA, Buhl wouldn't have been so fortunate.

Since Big Steve was still in Chicago and one day I had use of a free phone call to the States, I figured I'd get some first-hand information about our favorites. I placed the call so that it would be noon Chicago time and made a perfect connection. Unfortunately, Steve's octogenarian grandmother, who couldn't speak very much English, answered the phone. I asked her if Steve were there. Yes, she told me, but he was asleep, I should call back. Wait, I told her, I was calling from London, England; I wouldn't be able to call back. Could she please wake him up? No, she said, Stevie needed his sleep, she wouldn't wake him. I wanted to ask him about the Cubs, I said. "Cubs, phooey!" Steve's grandmother replied, and before I could plead any longer, she hung up on me.

I listened to the '65 World Series on the Armed Forces Radio Network in London with my friend Victor Holchak, a six-foot, five-inch ex-ballplayer from Los Angeles, who was then a student at the Royal Academy of Dramatic Art. The Dodgers, with Koufax striking out 29 Twins in 24 innings, took the Series. Why couldn't the Cubs have discovered Koufax? I asked Vic. "What would it have mattered?" he said. "They would have traded him away before he developed anyway."

THIRTY-SIX

In 1966 Leo Durocher was hired to manage the Cubs. The Lip hadn't had charge of a major league club since his third place 1955 New York Giant team. Since that time he'd served as a coach with the Dodgers but had been in the news more for his friendship with well-known entertainers such as Frank Sinatra than for any exploits on the diamond.

While Durocher was getting his lumps that first season he was in Chicago, I was organizing baseball games played with cricket bats and tennis balls behind the King's College Chapel at Cambridge University in England. Even though the professional urge had left me, I still retained enough of an ache for what I was so used to doing that during my brief tenure as a student in Cambridge I gathered together those few fellows—women included—who knew something of the sport, along with several who had not the slightest inkling of it, for what turned out to be a number of very spirited, if not entirely correct, baseball games. Each game drew quite a little crowd of spectators, many of whom applauded at inappropriate moments or failed to acknowledge those few well-executed maneuvers deserving of same.

At any rate, those makeshift games in Cambridge were certainly more enjoyable for me than the so-called professional endeavors engaged in by the Chicago club of the National League must have been for Leo the Lip. Under Durocher's guidance the Cubs lost 103 games in '66 and—contrary to the wishful thinking of 1962—finished dead last, tenth behind both Houston and the New York Mets.

Nineteen sixty-six was once again a pitcher's year. Sandy Koufax, for the first season in five, failed to pitch a no-hitter, but won 27 games nevertheless. Juan Marichal won 25; Gaylord Perry and Bob Gibson, 21 each; Chris Short of Philadelphia, an even 20. Dick Ellsworth, in what was to prove his final season in Cub mufti, *lost* 22. (He won 8.)

I wasn't there to witness it, but I don't imagine it was a pretty thing to watch. Big Steve, whose presence in the bleachers that season was no doubt as difficult as ever for the players to ignore, later told me that Ron Santo, recognizing Steve on the street after a game, tried to run him over with his car. At first I was inclined to write that story off as apocryphal but upon reconsideration concluded that I'd forgotten both how abrasive Big Steve's taunts could be and how terribly the Cubs were capable of playing. Since Santo led the league that season in errors and impressed Durocher as something less than a godsend of a clutch hitter, my tendency is to lean toward acceptance of Steve's version of the incident.

Despite Beckert and Kessinger's improvement of their averages to .287 and .274 respectively, Santo and Williams's big sticks (94 and 91 RBI), and the acquisition of catcher Randy Hundley, who hit 19 home runs, the Cubs were helpless. Not one pitcher had a good year; the staff ERA was 4.33, worst in the National League. The single bright light was a twenty-two-year-old black Canadian right-hander named Ferguson Jenkins who joined the team early in the season and finished 6 and 8 with a team-leading 3.32 ERA. He pitched very well at times, but his effort was often wasted because of a lack of support. It's doubtful, considering the Cub circumstances of 1966, that Jenkins could have predicted he would win 20 games or better each year for the next six years, or foreseen that before he was through he would win more than one hundred games in each of the major leagues.

"They still do play a World Series, don't they?" said P. K. Wrigley on May 14, 1966. "It's been so long I don't remember."

THIRTY-SEVEN

If by the end of 1966, having turned my attentions elsewhere, I wasn't much concerned with the doings of major league baseball, by the 1967 season I was practically unaware that such a thing existed. My temporary divorce from the heat of the professional sporting wars in America was a necessary happenstance. I needed time to clear—or, more correctly—becloud my head. I had, like any All-American boy, overdosed on sports, particularly baseball. I stopped reading the two-day-old line scores in the *International Herald Tribune* (which had absorbed the Paris edition of the *Times*); for the first time in a dozen years I did not first check to see if Willie Mays had hit a home run or stolen a base before reading the front-page headlines.

The only sports event to which I paid the least attention was the World Cup Football (soccer) Championship of '66, which was held in England. One could hardly ignore it, as every pub had its telly tuned to the match of the moment and literally every British citizen seemed obsessed by the fact of England's being in the finals for the first time in years past memory. I got a bit caught up in it and watched England defeat West Germany in the final match to take the cup. My friend Vic Holchak had been closely following the entire tournament—we watched the final together in his girl friend's flat on Priory Road in West Hampstead, London—and likened several of the participants to American baseball stars.

"Eusebio," Vic told me, referring to the brilliant black Por-

Ferguson Jenkins (Courtesy of George Brace)

tuguese wing from Mozambique, "is just like Hank Aaron. And Bobby Charlton is the British Stan Musial."

Friends like Vic made it difficult for me to forget from whence I'd come, but I had other friends, and I did my best to avoid news from the baseball front. Because of this I had no idea of the resurrection being accomplished in Chicago, that in 1967 the Cubs finished third behind St. Louis and San Francisco, 13 games over .500, and that Wrigley Field had begun to accommodate more than a million fans a year.

As is usually the case, pitching made the difference. The Dodgers, having lost Sandy Koufax forever with an arthritic elbow, faded fast to eighth place while the Cubs, behind Fergie Jenkins, who won 20, with a 2.80 ERA, southpaw Ken Holtzman, who, on a part-time basis (he was in the Army reserves and so could pitch only when he got a weekend pass), was 9 and 0 with a 2.53 ERA, Joe Niekro (10 wins), and ex–University of California star Rich Nye (13 wins), improved on their 1966 record by 18 games.

Ernie Banks, ever the marvel, and smelling a World Series for the first time in his long career, drove in 95 runs; Santo drove home 98 while batting .300, with 31 homers. Williams did the usual. Durocher was the toast of the town.

THIRTY-EIGHT

The Cardinals, led by that tireless performer and erstwhile Cub Louis Brock, won the National League pennant again in 1968; again the Giants finished second, and again the Cubs landed third. Jenkins, still in the early stage of his phenomenal streak, won 20 games; Bill Hands, a bullpen star of '67, won 16; Niekro won 14; and Phil Regan, stolen from L.A., saved 25. The unbelievable, irrepressible Banks hit 32 home runs. Glenn Beckert batted .294. Billy Williams did the usual. Outfielder Lou Johnson, the Cub spring training phenom of 1960 who had starred for the Dodgers in two World Series, returned to the Cubs for half a season and provided several clutch pinch hits. The Cubs were now the genuine article, an established threat to take the pennant. And they drew over a million again.

I returned to the States for good in '68 and settled in San Francisco, where I'd spent five months the previous year. I went to one night game at Candlestick Park with some friends who were not really baseball fans and knew nothing of my previous involvement with the game. The Candlestick wind was practically unbearable, and I discovered that it was difficult to concentrate on the action while freezing to death. I smoked a joint just before the first inning and it was the seventh before I realized that the second baseman wasn't Bobby Avila, a Cleveland Indian star of the 1950s. For the first few innings I was seeing ghosts. I felt lost at Candlestick, which could in no way be confused with the friendly confines of Wrigley Field. And what was Willie

Mays doing playing in a place like this? Ray Sadecki, the former St. Louis star, was pitching for the Giants, and a guy behind me kept shouting to him to "give 'im the dipsy-doo, Ray, the dipsy-doo." I was obviously still disaffected, I was stoned, but something more was wrong. Baseball was never meant to be played on a windy peninsula in forty-degree weather.

That night I had a dream in which I was a little boy riding in the backseat of my parents' car. It was a sunny Sunday afternoon in June and we were driving on a two-lane highway surrounded by cornfields on our way to Ray Radigan's Restaurant in Racine, Wisconsin. The Cub game was on the radio and Ernie Banks hit one high in the air toward center. A breeze came up and caught the ball just right, carrying it over the ivy into the center-field bleachers for a home run. When I woke up the next morning I remembered what I'd dreamed but I was certain it had really happened—not the night before but when I was eight or nine years old. Still, how could I be sure? More than the game had gotten away from me.

THIRTY-NINE

In 1969 the National and American Leagues divided themselves into two divisions each, East and West. The Cubs were lumped in the East with Pittsburgh, St. Louis, Philadelphia, Montreal, Atlanta, and New York. It seemed obvious that if they could get by the Pirates, Cards, and Phillies, the division would be theirs. It seemed that way, and in this first season of obligatory demarcation they did just what they had to in order to win by finishing ahead—by a comfortable margin—of those three most formidable divisional rivals. What nobody counted on, however, was the Mets, the Amazin' Mets, as they came to be called. That season the Mets won 100 games, the Eastern Division title, and then, in the first Championship Series ever played, defeated the Western Division leaders, the Atlanta Braves, for the pennant.

The point to be made here is that for all practical purposes the Cubs had the division wrapped and they blew it. I was living that year in the wilderness just below the Oregon border, and baseball news was scarce. In August, however, when I saw in a day-old *San Francisco Chronicle* that the Cubs were in first place, I began to check a newspaper every couple of days. The news I got was incomplete, of course, but as it turned out strange things were happening. Right in the middle of the pennant race, manager Leo Durocher took an unauthorized vacation to be with his son at summer camp in Wisconsin. (A truly great coincidence: the campground was in Eagle River—the same I'd attended in 1955!) Why he did this I don't have any idea, but it seemed that from that point on, the Cubs lost ground steadily to the Mets.

My baseball interest had begun to revive. I was, certainly, thrilled that Ernie Banks might finally make it to a World Series in uniform, and other things were happening that intrigued me. Reggie Jackson, a young Oakland outfielder, hit something like 40 home runs in the first half of the season; Steve Carlton of St. Louis struck out 19 batters in a nine-inning game, breaking Bob Feller's ("Bob Rapid," Satchel Paige called him) thirty-one-year-old record of 18; Pete Rose, the Cincinnati player I'd tabbed as something special back when he was averaging .265, hit .348 to win his second straight batting title; the American League seemed to be on a home run binge, ending up with five players having 40 or more—Jackson finished with 47, *third* in the league behind Frank Howard's 48 and Harmon "the Killer" Killebrew's 49. The game was beginning to work its magic on me again. I'd needed that time off from it in order to renew my perspective, and my personal revival had happened at exactly the right moment, just as the Cubs were about to win their first pennant since the year before I was born. At least that's what I thought.

Ernie Banks did all he could to bring the flag to Chicago in '69. At the age of thirty-eight he hit 23 homers and drove in 106 runs in 155 games. Ron Santo hit 29 out and drove in a career-high 123; Glenn Beckert batted .291; Jim Hickman hit 21 home runs; Fergie won 21; Hands won 20; Holtzman won 17. And Sweet Billy did the usual.

But none of it, alas, was enough. It was the Year of the Mets, who went on to defeat a powerful Baltimore Oriole team in the World Series 4 games to 1. The Mets, who had been in the National League only since 1962. The Cubs, though, had gone from tenth place to second in their division in three seasons. Except for Banks, who was eternally youthful, it was still a young team. The Mets had won, proving thereby that anything was possible.

FORTY

Between the ages of eight and fifteen, during those months the weather would permit it—and often when I chose to ignore its dictates—I spent at least two hours a day bouncing a ball against the yellow brick wall of the garage behind my house. Like Dorothy following the yellow brick road, I threw each successive ball in an ascending series, tracking the pattern the bricks made toward the roof of the garage. I played game after game like that, using either a tennis ball or a hard ball and my fielder's glove, pretending I was Carrasquel, Aparicio, or Banks, Billy Cox (my first third-base idol), or Johnny Logan—I was always, except for that one year I played left field for Royal Awning, an infielder —or any of a dozen other ballplayers I admired. I hit the ball off the wall at every conceivable angle, practicing with my eyes closed, depending on the *sound* of the rebound, even diving on the cement to snag a wayward bounce, hoping it wouldn't kick off a crack in the cement and bound up into my face.

When I was eleven I accidentally left my Billy Martin model mitt out overnight. It rained heavily, and when I looked out my back window the next morning and saw it lying there my heart jumped into my throat and gagged me. I ran out and picked it up and of course it was ruined. The leather was so soggy that the laces just fell apart in my hand. I didn't want my mother to know I'd been so careless about taking care of my glove and that it was ruined, so I carried it into the alley and dumped it into a neighbor's garbage can. Then I went into my house and dug my collection of silver dollars out of the bottom drawer of my dresser, walked down to Hobbymodels sporting goods store on Western Avenue, and bought a Bill Tuttle model fielder's glove. Tuttle was an outfielder with Kansas City then, not a bad one, but what I would have preferred to buy was a Frank Bolling model with the enlarged web, recessed pocket, and extended fingers. The difference in price between the Tuttle and Bolling models was about twenty dollars, so I had to settle for the Tuttle. As the silver dollars represented my life's savings to that point it was a major purchase, tantamount to an adult's buying an automobile. I spent the necessary hours working in the new glove, oiling it carefully, keeping it tied up with a ball in the pocket. The Tuttle model worked out all right but I missed my Billy Martin—no glove I've had since has folded over the ball precisely the way that one did. My mother never found out what happened to it.

When two or three years later I saw Billy Martin, then with the Cincinnati Reds, punch Cub pitcher Jim Brewer in the face, breaking his cheekbone,* on the mound at Wrigley Field, I thought about my old glove and how awful I'd felt holding it in my hands that morning after the rain. But not until 1969 did I dwell on it again. It was October, just after the World Series, and I was lying in bed late at night when I heard the first drops of rain since June falling on the roof of my house in the country. Gradually the rain intensified, and for whatever reason the image of my waterlogged Billy Martin model baseball glove came into my head. Baseball, it occurred to me at that moment, was a true love. I would never abandon it again.

---

*In his book, *Number 1*, Martin claims that it was actually Cincinnati pitcher Cal McLish who landed the damaging blow.

FORTY-ONE

By 1970 it was becoming obvious that the Cubs were in a kind of rut, a mild one, perhaps, but a rut nevertheless. As a manager, Durocher had welded the team into a solid contender, and because of this Ernie Banks clung to the hope of finally appearing in a World Series, staying on the active list and contributing, despite his displacement at first base by Jim Hickman. Banks performed on a par with high-priced acquisitions Johnny Callison and Joe Pepitone, but once again it was to no avail. The Cubs finished second in the East, five games behind Pittsburgh.

The 1970 season was the one Curt Flood, the All-Star St. Louis outfielder who refused to report to the Phillies, to whom he'd been traded, sat out while battling the reserve clause in the courts. Though he lost his case, it would, of course, eventually serve to alter forever the chattel-like control management had kept over players since the beginning of professional baseball; it would also do much to change the nature of the fans' association with their hometown heroes. The notion of "hometown" swiftly becoming an archaic curiosity insofar as players' allegiance was concerned. Though the Cub ownership would not plunge into the free-agent market as readily as some other clubs, changes in its heretofore conservative policies were inevitable.

Also in 1970, on the playing field, Cesar Gutierrez, a .240-hitting Detroit shortstop, in what would be his only full season in the majors, became the first player in modern history to collect 7 consecutive hits in one game, the feat not having been accomplished since 1892. Tom Seaver of the Mets (who finished one game back of the Cubs) matched Steve Carlton's 19 strikeouts in a nine-inning game, striking out 10 Padre batters in a row to set a new record in that department. Hank Aaron and Willie Mays each got their 3,000th hit, and it began to appear a reality that Bad Henry might just be the man to surpass Babe Ruth in the all-time homer category.

But the most outstanding statistic for 1970 concerned a Cub, Billy Williams, who, while accomplishing considerably *more* than the usual—compiling 42 home runs, 129 RBI, and scoring a league-leading 137 runs while batting .322—sat out a game, the first such occurrence for him in the last 1,118 Cub contests, thereby putting to an end the longest iron-man streak in National League history and third-longest in the history of major league baseball. I realized that I had been privileged to have beheld in my relatively brief lifetime two Cub players, Billy Williams and Ernie Banks, destined for the Hall of Fame. The one sad note about this, of course, was that Williams, like Banks, would never have the privilege of playing in a World Series.

The Cubs did well in '70, staying in contention most of the way. Jenkins turned in 22 victories; Jim Hickman had the biggest season of his baseball life, batting .315, with 32 homers and 115 RBI; Santo knocked in 114; Beckert hit .288; and then there was that left fielder from Whistler, Alabama, who, though he had to take a short rest, performed creditably.

There was nothing really wrong with the Cubs, but Pittsburgh, with Roberto the Great hitting .352, was better; and even the Pirates could not compete in the play-off for the pennant with Cincinnati's four .300 hitters and Johnny Bench, who for the season batted .293, along with his major-league-leading 45 home runs and 148 RBI. It's doubtful whether the Cubs were better even than Los Angeles or San Francisco, both of whom won more games that season. The Cubs weren't bad, they just weren't good enough.

FORTY-TWO

Big Steve had moved to Los Angeles in 1969, so, since I was living in San Francisco, we were able to see one another more often than when he was back in Chicago. In May of 1970 I went down to see him and we spent an afternoon at Chavez Ravine watching the Dodgers play the Pirates. I liked Dodger Stadium's simplicity and was amused by the fact that most of the enormous Saturday afternoon crowd of 50,000 seemed to be from New York, Chicago, or Union City, New Jersey. All of them were rabid Dodger fans, a condition that both shocked and horrified me. Big Steve hated the Dodgers, too, an attitude that he maintains to this day. Also to his credit, though he now lives in New York City, is that he finds it impossible to root for either the Yankees or the Mets. He is a Cub fan to the bone.

Steve's passion for the Cubs has been rivaled only by his affection for the race track. Since the age of fifteen Big Steve has been an ardent handicapper, consistently turning a fair profit for the season. Part of the reason for his success has been his fearless attitude toward betting. When we were sixteen I watched him put two hundred dollars on the nose on Tom Rolfe in the feature at Arlington Park, a considerable amount for one of us to wager in those days. Throughout the race Steve kept a straight face, showing no emotion, and when the little horse poked his head forward at the wire right in front of us to take the race by a nostril Steve didn't say a word, just smiled and walked calmly to the pay window.

He wasn't always so successful, however. When he was at the University of Illinois I drove up to Champaign from Missouri and picked him up the night before the Kentucky Derby. We had decided to pool our resources and have a big weekend in Louisville. That night I got drunk and Steve had to drive almost all the way in my 1955 maroon Buick Century dressed in a wet tuxedo while I slept it off in the backseat. While I had been off drinking beer Big Steve had gone to a formal party of some kind where he had somehow managed to get thrown into a swimming pool.

We arrived in Louisville just as the sun was coming up and drove directly to Churchill Downs. Steve took advantage of the sun to stand against the car and let his tuxedo dry. There was already a crowd collecting and the morning broke balmy and beautiful, an ideal day for the Derby.

As it turned out, however, it was less than an idyll for us. By Derby time, which was the eighth race, Steve had dropped over two hundred and I'd lost about one and a quarter. Between us we had a hundred and a half left, and we put it down across the board on the favorite, a Chicago-owned animal whose name I prefer to forget. So as not to prolong what for me is an agonizing memory, I'll just say that not only did the favorite lose but he did not get a call after the back stretch. As the race finished, a man standing in front of me who had several tickets on the winner leaped up and down, shouting in delight. In his excitement he threw all of his tickets in the air. As he stooped to retrieve them I carefully covered one with my foot. He never missed it, picked up the others, and ran to collect. After the crowd dispersed I bent down and picked it up: a two-dollar win ticket that would pay seven-forty. I was completely broke, as was Steve, and the seven bucks would buy us gas to get home. Our big weekend plans had finished back in the pack.

I cashed in the ticket and as we were leaving the track Big Steve stopped in front of a crippled and blind man on the ground outside the gate who was selling pencils for five cents apiece. Steve reached in his pocket, turned it inside out, and extracted the total contents, a nickel. He flipped the coin into the crippled man's hat. "Keep the pencil," he said.

We bought seven dollars' worth of gas and I drove until we were about a half hour outside of Champaign, where I got out to take a leak and let Steve take over the wheel. It was a little after ten o'clock at night, and I went to sleep in the back. About two hours later I awoke to find us speeding along an unlit two-lane highway surrounded by wheat fields.

"Where are we?" I asked Steve. "We should have been in Champaign an hour and a half ago."

"I think I took a wrong turn," said Big Steve.

I spotted a one-pump country filling station just ahead and ordered Steve to pull in there. I got out and asked the attendant if we were in Illinois. We were not. Illinois was back the other way. We were somewhere in the middle of Indiana. Without a word Steve climbed into the backseat and went to sleep. Since the tank was close to empty I used our last forty cents for gas and prayed we'd make it. We did, and I fell asleep in the car about two seconds after I pulled up in front of Steve's house. When I woke up in the morning Big Steve was gone and there was a five-dollar bill on the dashboard, which I used to buy gas, then I drove back to Missouri.

I reminded Steve of this particular adventure that day at Dodger Stadium in 1970, adding that it had occurred exactly five years before to the day.

"I'm glad you mentioned it," he said. "You never did pay me back that five bucks."

FORTY-THREE

Ernie Banks played his final season for the Cubs in 1971. He was forty years old, and the team finished tied for third in their division, 14 games behind Pittsburgh. Banks appeared only 39 times and had a total of 83 at bats. His 16 hits included 3 home runs, which tied him for ninth place on the all-time list. Eddie Mathews had retired three years earlier, but I expected that he might make a belated comeback, hit one more homer, and retire again, just so he could be one ahead of Ernie. In nineteen years Banks played in 2,528 regular season games, none in post-season action.

The fans came out to watch, as they always did these days, and saw Glenn Beckert mature into a .342 hitter. Ex-Yankee Joe Pepitone, wearing a different toupee for each day of the week (he would later go on to another kind of fame as a nude centerfold in *Foxy Lady* magazine), had a good year, batting .307, with 16 home runs. Santo and Hickman tailed off, but Billy the Smooth added 28 home runs and 93 RBI to another .300 season. Fergie finally won the Cy Young Award as the National League's leading pitcher, compiling 24 wins and a remarkable 2.77 ERA. For any pitcher to allow fewer than 3 runs per game is outstanding, but to accomplish it while pitching a majority of the time in a home run hitter's paradise like Wrigley Field is practically a miracle. Jenkins's achievement of having won more than 100 games in both major leagues is particularly amazing because of his lengthy tenure in Wrigley Field and his two seasons in Boston's Fenway Park, due to the friendly batter's breezes and short fences the two most unenviable sites in which a major league pitcher might toil. Fergie's 1971 performance was further enhanced by his unexpected dexterity with the bat, hitting 6 home runs and driving home 20.

Milt Pappas, the former Oriole whiz, won 17 games (he would be the only pitcher in major league history to win more than 200 games while never having a 20-game win season), but both Holtzman and Hands showed won-lost records well below .500. Durocher talked increasingly of the old days in New York with Willie Mays, who in '71 helped San Francisco to the Western Division title. By the next year Mays would be back in New York, with the Mets, and Leo would have freed himself so that he might spend as much time with his son as he chose.

In the Bay Area I watched the rise of Finley's A's, led by ex–Red Sox manager Dick Williams, the team that would dominate baseball in the early and mid-'70s. Chicago seemed far away and headed farther down in the standings. Why hadn't they been the ones to have come up with Vida Blue? I asked myself, forgetting momentarily Vic Holchak's assessment of a similar postulation I'd made regarding Sandy Koufax. And what would Wrigley Field be like without Ernie Banks?

FORTY-FOUR

The 1972 season was more of the same except that this time the Cubs finished second, 11 games back, and a frustrated Durocher dropped out after 90 official contests, being replaced as manager by Whitey Lockman, who had been the first baseman on Leo the Lip's 1954 World Championship New York Giants team. Pittsburgh again took the division, with the great Roberto Clemente batting .312, his thirteenth season over .300. Of Clemente's 118 hits that season, the last would be not only the 3,000th of his career but the last he would ever have the opportunity of stroking. On New Year's Eve he would be killed in a plane crash. Of my earliest boyhood heroes only Hank Aaron and Willie Mays were still active as players. Ted Williams, Musial, Banks, and now Clemente were gone.

Billy Williams led the majors in '72 with a .333 batting average that included 37 homers and 122 RBI. Incredibly, he was not voted the Most Valuable Player Award, that distinction going to the Reds' catcher Johnny Bench, who had also won it in 1970. Bench had a great season, too, of course, hitting 40 home runs, but he had the added virtue of playing with a pennant-winning team, a situation that has often proved the difference in close balloting for the MVP. Playing for the Cubs did little to improve Billy Williams's fortune, a fact that would have won him my vote even if Bench—who was certainly just as deserving of the award—had hit 50 home runs. Only Ernie Banks, now a Cub batting coach, had been able to consistently distinguish himself from his mediocre teammates in the eyes of the baseball writers when he won those two consecutive Most Valuable Player awards in '58 and '59. Sweet Billy deserved better. Perhaps his quiet, outwardly calm demeanor did him a disservice in this regard.

Lockman improved only slightly on the Lip's record that year, and outside of Williams only outfielder Jose Cardenal accomplished anything of note with the stick, batting .291, with 17 homers. Fergie won 20 for the sixth year in a row; because he played in Chicago, he complained, and not in New York or Los Angeles, nobody knew who he was. If not "nobody," certainly not enough fans were aware of his remarkable record. Ed Kranepool, for example, the Mets' first baseman, who at that point in his career carried an approximate .250 lifetime average, was easily a player better known to the public than Jenkins, primarily—if not only—because he played in New York. Jenkins would not have to wait long before being granted his wish to leave Chicago, but, as he was to discover, Texas—his first stop—was not New York either.

Right-hander Rick Reuschel made his entrance with the Cubs in '72, winning 10 games with a 2.93 ERA; and Burt Hooton, he of knuckle-curve fame, became a starting pitcher, posting a fine 2.80 ERA that belied his 11 and 14 won-lost mark. Laboring in the Cub farm system and about to quit baseball was Bruce Sutter, soon to come under the tutelage of minor league pitching instructor Freddie Martin, who would provide Sutter with the knowledge necessary to the throwing of a pitch even more devastating to batters than either Hooton's knuckle-curve or ex-Pirate Roy Face's fork ball: a fast fork ball that in Sutter's repertoire would prove to be virtually unhittable. Sutter, however, was still four years from the majors and the immediate outlook for the Cubs was as bleak as it had been for years.

FORTY-FIVE

By 1973 the Cubs, under a full season with Lockman at the helm, were down to fifth place in the East. In what was to be his last season, Willie Mays went to the World Series with the Mets—who lost to Oakland—the second pennant they'd won in five years, a fact long-time and long-suffering Cub fans could hardly help but lose some sleep over. The Cubs had a chance to take the division, but they faded along with St. Louis, Pittsburgh, and Montreal. (Even the fledgling Expos had overtaken them!) New York finished the regular season only 3 games over .500, then beat heavily-favored Cincinnati in the play-offs for another Met miracle.

Ferguson Jenkins finished 14 and 16—not even he could win 20 with this year's club. Cardenal hit .303. Rick Monday, who had been acquired the previous season from Oakland for Ken Holtzman, had his second disappointing year in a Cubbie suit, following up a .249 average with a .267 while Holtzman won 19 for the A's in '72 and 21 in '73. (Monday's most spectacular performance as a Cub came when he wrested an American flag from a crazed spectator on the field one day—a game at which Big Steve was in attendance.) Thirty-five-year-old Billy Williams hit .288, 20 home runs, and drove in 86. There was no joy in Cubville.

Two-thirds of the way through the next season Whitey Lockman gave way to Jim Marshall, an ex-Cub player, who could do no better as the Cubs fell to sixth, last in the Eastern Division. Beginning in the late '60s, they'd had their run, and were now back in more familiar territory. Their top starter, Bill Bonham, lost 22 times; Reuschel wound up with a 4.29 ERA. The staff ERA was 4.28, lowest in the National League except for expansion club San Diego's.

Third baseman Bill Madlock, obtained from Texas in the trade for Jenkins, hit .313, and would prove to be worth the price. Even though Fergie won 25 games for the Rangers in 1974, most in the majors, Madlock would go on to win two consecutive National League batting titles in the next two seasons. Other Cub highlights of '74 were Jose Cardenal's consistency—.293 average, 72 RBI—and Rick Monday's .294 mark. Monday led the league in double plays for an outfielder with 5, a possibly dubious distinction, since enemy base runners obviously felt that they could take liberties with his arm.

The real highlights of 1974 were in other arenas. Detroit's Al Kaline, the youngest player in Major League history ever to have won a batting title (.340 in 1955, when he was twenty), ripped his 3,000th safety to join company with Clemente, Musial, Cobb, Hornsby, and the several other immortals who'd accomplished the feat. Hank Aaron, one of those several, became even more immortal(!) by breaking Babe Ruth's "unbeatable" all-time home run record, swatting his 715th round-tripper on national television in a game at his home stadium in Atlanta; the next year he would be a designated hitter for the Brewers back in Milwaukee, where—for Aaron—it had all begun.

And Lou Brock, the same whom ten seasons earlier the Cubs had eagerly exchanged for a sore-armed pitcher now eight years to pasture, set an all-time Major League record for stolen bases with 118, breaking Maury Wills's "unbeatable" 1962 record of 104; Brock, who had 194 hits and drew 88 walks while batting .306, was thirty-five years old.

The 1975 season proved no better for the Cubs as they finished last again, tied with the Expos. Madlock won the first of his two titles, batting .354. Cardenal hit .317 and announced his displeasure with the geography; he'd seen what had happened to Ernie. Cardenal wanted out of Chicago, he wanted to play with a winner. Bill Bonham lost only 15 games in '75, but Reuschel dropped a league-leading 17. The team ERA was 4.52; no other National League pitching staff even came close to being that bad (San Diego, 1974's worst, was better than the Cubs' '75 mark by more than a run). Billy Williams was not in Chicago, however, playing the first of his two final seasons in the majors for the Oakland A's, for whom he hit 23 homers and drove in 81 runs. Unfortunately for Billy, the A's were just past their prime, and though he helped them gain the Championship Play-offs, they didn't quite have the talent to take the pennant, and that was the closest Williams would come to the October classic.

But the biggest news in baseball during this dismal "return to normalcy" for the Cubs was that Curt Flood's challenge to the reserve clause had borne fruit. Due to a provision in his contract that owner Charlie Finley had failed to honor, Oakland star pitcher Catfish Hunter was able to lease his services to the highest bidder, the New York Yankees, for several million dollars. Angel hurler Andy Messersmith was declared a free agent and hied himself off to Atlanta for even bigger bucks (though he, too —as well as Reggie Jackson, Oscar Gamble, Don Gullet, Goose Gossage, and numerous others—would eventually end up with the Yankees); and Pirate outfielder Richie Zisk, like Oriole pitcher Wayne Garland, would deal himself away for what amounted to a lifetime contract for what appeared to the average fan an astronomical sum. New York Yankee owner George Steinbrenner, along with Anaheim's Gene Autry, Atlanta's Ted Turner, and Texas's Brad Corbett, broke down all barriers regarding limits to what an owner might pay a ballplayer for his services. As is usually the case in these situations, the man who made instant fortunes possible for so many of his kind, Curt Flood, made nothing on any of these deals. By 1980, at the age of forty-two and claiming he could still make it in the majors if someone would give him a chance, he would be playing third base on a coed slow-pitch softball team in Oakland.

FORTY-SIX

One November night in 1975 when I was in New York City my friend Marshall and I went into Donohue's on Seventy-second Street to have a beer. It was a cold night but I felt like a beer in an Irish bar and Donohue's was on the way home. Marshall said they served good dinners but I wasn't hungry yet, I wanted to eat at La Maravilla anyway (this was before that establishment's unfortunate decline), so we figured we'd have a couple, then walk up to Eighty-fifth and have some *ropa vieja*.

We were about to leave when a guy midway down the bar began talking Cuban English loud enough for us to hear. He was telling baseball stories, but I couldn't tell who he was, I'd missed his name if he'd said it. He was wearing a belted trenchcoat, all lapels and buttons, and used a high-pitched Desi Arnaz laugh to punctuate his speedy patter. He ordered vodka with an orange juice chaser. I went over and asked him his name.

"Willie Miranda!"

"Oh sure, I remember you," I said.

He smiled and nodded rapidly. "Sure you remember me, Willie Miranda, you remember me."

"I saw you when you were with the White Sox, and with Baltimore. You were a great fielder."

Still nodding and smiling, he said, "I was pret' goo' heeter, too. I drove een only ron when Weel-helm peetch hees no-heet gen New York. I know McDougal' at thir' take too moch time throw to firs', so I heet groun' ball to heem weeth man on thir' and beet eet out."*

"That was in 1958," I said.

"Ha ha!" He slapped me on the back. "He know more than you guys," he said to the others at the bar. "Nineteen feefty-eight, you remember!

"But no more Cuban ballplayers now," he said. "Minoso, Luis Aloma, Arroyo."

"Sandy Consuegra," I added. "He won sixteen one year for the Sox. And Carlos Paula, with the Senators. He kept getting hit in the head with fly balls."

Willie nodded. "Tony Taylor the las' one lef'."

"How about El Tiante and Tony Perez?" I said.

"Yeah, yeah," he agreed, "them too."

He took a sip of the vodka. "I leev now een the Bronx weeth Cepeda's seester. I look for chob as maître d'. I bin work at Playboy Club, checkin' keys. But I was fire'. I'm wait now for check, thousan' dollar, after tha' nothing, but I ain' worry. People remember Willie Miranda."

He finished off the vodka. His stiff black pompadour was streaked with gray. He was about twenty pounds overweight for his five feet nine inches.

"Castro ruin Cuba," he said. "Ain' nothin' for people there now."

"They're eating," I said. "They're healthier, the literacy rate is up. And Castro was a ballplayer, they have a great amateur team."

"Sure, Cubans the bes' ballplayers! But they ain' nothin' there." He shook his head. "No money, no decen' life."

He ordered another drink. Marshall was moving toward the door. I zipped up my jacket.

"Nice to have met you, Willie," I said. "Good luck."

---

*Regarding Hoyt Wilhelm's no-hitter for Baltimore vs. New York in 1958, American League records show that the only run scored in the game was on a seventh-inning home run into the left-center field bleachers by Oriole catcher Gus Triandos off Yankee relief pitcher Bobby Shantz.

He drank half the vodka quickly and nodded. "Sure, sure," he said, as we shook hands. "I be all ri', everybody remember Willie Miranda."

<small>POSTSCRIPT:</small> On July 15, 1980, in a game against the New York Yankees, a utility infielder for the Minnesota Twins turned a sure-hit bouncer up the middle into an out with a bare-handed grab and throw. After the game, Minnesota manager Gene Mauch, a veteran of four major league decades, commented, "That's a play you'd expect Willie Miranda to make."

FORTY-SEVEN

The Cubs did a little bit better in 1976, finishing fourth. Bill Madlock hit .339 and led the league again. Cardenal hit .299. Rick Monday hit 32 home runs. The big news in Chicago, though, was Bruce Sutter, who had finally surfaced with the monster fork ball, the pitch that by 1979 would win him the Cy Young Award and a contract guaranteeing him—for one season, anyway—the most money ever paid to a relief pitcher in the history of baseball.

In his first season Sutter was 6 and 3 with an ERA of 2.71. The combined figures for his first four years in the majors, all with the Cubs, showed a 27 and 22 won-lost count, 418 strikeouts in 390 innings (against 115 bases on balls), and a 2.33 ERA. The fast fork ball confounded everybody, giving the illusion of being a very hittable pitch at the knees until the last instant, breaking down sharply as it crossed the plate. "Most of the time they'd be called balls," admitted Sutter, "if the batters would only leave 'em alone." But the batters didn't, and Sutter was virtually untouchable.

Other than the emergence of Superman Sutter the Cubs had little to crow about. Elsewhere, Hammerin' Hank retired with 755 home runs, 6,856 total bases, 1,477 extra base hits, and 3,297 RBI to his credit, each a Major League record. He had also played in more games—3,298—than anybody else, come to bat more times (12,364), pounded out 3,771 hits (second only to Tyrus Cobb's "unbeatable" 4,191), and cracked 624 doubles, only good enough for sixth on the all-time list. I felt privileged to have witnessed more than a few of each of those, including his 715th home run, but the memory of a twenty-year-old Aaron, hitting one off the center-field ivy in Wrigley Field in 1954, *wristing* it with a *snap* I swore I could hear, remains my favorite recollection of him. As an eight-year-old I adopted his original batting stance, a cobra posture, rear end extended, wrists cocked, bat tilted slightly forward. He expressed his philosophy of hitting succinctly: "I see the ball, I hit the ball." Hank Aaron was the last of my early heroes to hang 'em up. It was difficult for me to believe that he'd played for twenty-three years, a calculation that made a reality out of the even greater imponderable that I must therefore be more than thirty years old.

Another 1976 retiree was Billy Williams, Sweet Swinging Billy, who bade farewell to the bigs in Oakland, California, not Chicago, after 18 seasons (13 in a row with 20 or more home runs) and no Series ring. This, too, was the year Lou Brock, the man the Cubs could never forget, still in a Redbird uniform, batted .301—the sixth year out of the last seven that he'd exceeded the magic figure—and stole 50 bases for the twelfth straight season, a major league record.

FORTY-EIGHT

The next three years, 1977 through 1979, constituted the era of Herman Franks, who took over as manager from Jim Marshall. Hefty Herman, the real estate sharpie from Utah, had managed the San Francisco Giants to four straight Western Division second-place finishes from 1965 to 1968, and was perhaps best known for having acted as Willie Mays's agent at the same time that he was managing him. Franks, however, got some new personnel to work with, and the Cubs made some noise in the National League for the first time since the Lip abandoned ship.

Rick Monday and pitcher Mike Garman were dispatched to L.A. in exchange for first baseman Bill Buckner and shortstop Ivan DeJesus, two quality players who produced immediate results, as did third baseman Steve Ontiveros, on whom the Giants had given up. Buckner batted .284 despite a bad ankle, and DeJesus .266 while fielding superbly, leading the majors in assists for shortstops with 595. I was surprised that the Dodgers were willing to part with either Buckner, with whom Los Angeles skipper Tom Lasorda had maintained a close relationship and promised never to trade, or DeJesus, who was vastly superior in the field to their current shortstop Bill Russell, and who promised to hit as well if not better and for more power. In any case, the deal was a steal for the Cubs as Garman didn't last long and Monday became a chronic injury case. Ontiveros was a complete and pleasant surprise, batting .299 and fielding adequately.

Ex-Yankee phenom Bobby Murcer, who'd come to the Cubs

with Ontiveros from San Francisco for batting champion Madlock—Madlock had wanted too much money, said the Wrigley organization, and that was always a cause for expulsion—blasted 27 homers and drove in 89 runs. Second baseman Manny Trillo hit well over .300 for most of the season and provided the other half of a successful double-play combination. Names like Biittner, Gross, Clines, and Morales registered over .290 in the Sunday averages. Rick Reuschel won 20 games despite his battle with the weight bug, and Bruce Sutter was simply unbelievable, picking up 31 saves while compiling a microscopic 1.35 ERA. The Cubs broke even, 81 and 81, fourth in the division, and the fans, seizing an all-too-rare opportunity, begged for more.

A large footnote to the '77 season was the Yankees' return to dominance, defeating the Dodgers in the World Series, just as they would the following year. In the sixth and final game, New York's Reggie Jackson earned the nickname "Mr. October" by blasting three consecutive home runs, each hit off the first pitch served up to him and each blasted successively farther than the last in what was probably the most impressive individual batting performance in Series history.

Even though they won fewer games in 1978, ending up below .500 at 79 and 83, the Cubs improved their standing in the National League East, moving up one notch from fourth to third. Ex-Giant, Met, Padre, Angel, and Yankee (did I miss any?) Dave "King Kong" Kingman, he of the prodigious home run and equally prodigious swish, joined the fold in '78 and bashed 28 homers in only 395 at bats. Great things were predicted for Kingman in Wrigley Field, the hive where big bats thrive. If he could only stay healthy and happy, wrote the local scribes, acknowledging that those were two mighty big ifs.

Most of the previous season's brigade of newcomers once again acquitted themselves admirably. Buckner led the team in hitting with .323, nearly leading the league, something he surely would have done had his now chronically sore ankle not prevented him from beating out infield hits. DeJesus improved his average to .278 and again led the majors in assists for a shortstop with 558. Manny Trillo topped all other National League second basemen in the same department, registering 505. Ontiveros, however, slumped because of injury, and Murcer's power quotient declined appreciably, giving rise to rumors regarding both of their expendability, especially Murcer's; by the following June Bobby was back with the Yankees.

Sutter had what was for him a mediocre season, as did Reuschel, but there were no trade rumors as yet involving them. (It would be a couple of years before Sutter began barking the Cardinal script.) Some young arms came to the fore, most notably Dennis Lamp and Mike Krukow. Franks was optimistic and predicted (shades of Bob Kennedy, who was by now the club's vice-president), barring injuries, a more sustained run at the money in 1979. The Cubs had become famous for showing good early foot, then falling back faster than a front runner Big Steve and I regularly used to lose money on at Arlington named Killoqua used to die at the wire. Killoqua would be right up there until the last few yards and then drop as suddenly and dramatically as if someone had plugged her with a bullet from the grandstand. By late August the Cubs, who had started out like Whirlaway, looked like a tired old Clydesdale. In 1969, 1973, and 1977 the Cubs were in first place on July 4, the traditional midway point of the season, only to finish second, fifth, and third, respectively.

Pete Rose, however, at thirty-seven, looked as strong as ever as he batted .302 and got *his* 3,000th hit. Now in a Phillie uniform, Charlie Hustle looked to me the same as he had in 1964 in Cincinnati, like a man who was out to win. Another man who was out to win in '78 was Yankee third baseman Graig Nettles, who made seven brilliant fielding plays as New York captured the Series again; four of Nettles' gems saved the third game for pitcher Ron Guidry, preventing, by my count, seven runs from scoring. Mr. October belted two homers and batted .391. The Dodgers won two games, and I couldn't help but wonder how an early-season version of the Cubs might have fared in their place.

FORTY-NINE

Despite Herman Franks's promises, the Cub team of 1979 was no different from those of the recent past, getting off to an impressive start and then having to fight for its life to finish around .500. The most memorable contest of the regular season was a 10-inning game played on May 17 against Philadelphia at Wrigley Field, which the Phillies, aided by that superb home run breeze, won by a score of 23 to 22! If the season represented no significant change for the Cubs as a whole, it could nevertheless be officially recorded as the year slugger Dave Kingman came of age as both a hitter and an outfielder.

Kingman, who had grown up near Chicago, had been a pitcher at the University of Southern California. While playing in college, Big Dave would regularly astound spectators with 500-foot drives into the ozone. "Nobody ever hit a ball farther than Kingman," said Vic Holchak, who'd seen him deposit several Pacific Athletic Conference horsehides on Mars. Until his 1979 season with Chicago, Kingman had been as famous for his numerous strikeouts (140 in '72, 153 in '75, 143 in '77 as only a part-time performer) as for his incredible clouts. There have been any number of heavy swatters—Dave Nicholson and Steve Bilko to name two of the more outstanding—who could never learn to cut down on their swing and thus never made it as the bona fide major league sluggers it was hoped they'd become. But in '79 Dave Kingman widened his stance and reduced the arc his bat made while following through, bringing his six-foot, six-inch

Lou Brock (Courtesy of St. Louis Cardinals)

frame more clearly within range of finding a ninety-mile-per-hour pitch and picking it out of the air with a thin piece of hardwood. His statistics tell the story: a .288 average (by far the highest of his career), 48 home runs, 115 RBI. Not only that, but he became a reliable left fielder, putting to rest the oft-heard Dr. Strangeglove handle originally the property of former Red Sox–Pirate–Phillie first baseman Dick Stuart.

Kingman's 1979 performance notwithstanding, as well as the usual professional support from Buckner, DeJesus, and Sutter—who struck out the entire world and copped the Cy Young—Herman Franks decided he'd had enough and retired following the season to the real estate wars. The year 1980 would dawn on Preston Gomez, the former San Diego and Houston pilot, as the new Cub manager. Gomez's efforts had not met with success at either of his previous venues and I doubted that he was the man to bring an end to the thirty-five-year famine, but I was willing to wait and see, just as I always had. Actually, I was annoyed that the Cub management had not seen fit to hire Baltimore coach Frank Robinson as skipper, Robby having proved his ability at Cleveland and in Puerto Rico; or Maury Wills, or anybody but one of the old guard that was part of the major leagues' musical chairs manager brigade. Especially now that old P. K. Wrigley had died, it seemed to me that William Wrigley, his son, who was now running the team, should be willing to try a new face, to step out a little. There was certainly little to lose by taking a chance.

As heartened as I truly had been by Dave Kingman's outstanding improvement in '79, I had to admit that the two most marvelous events of the baseball year—for me—had been Pete Rose's 44-game hitting streak, a new National League record, and Lou Brock's comeback season, his nineteenth and last in the big leagues.

In his final bow Brock ripped his 3,000th hit (Carl Yastrzemski did the same for Boston in what seemed to be a mild epidemic of extraordinary achievement), batted over .300 following a disastrous .221 in '78, and stole his 933rd base, breaking Billy Hamilton's nineteenth-century mark. Brock had suffered under the two-year reign of Cardinal manager Vern Rapp, who had insisted that Lou was washed up. But Brock fought back and blossomed anew after Rapp was dismissed (dissension on the squad was rife) and replaced by Brock's former teammate Ken Boyer. Boyer himself would not last past the early summer of 1980, but by then Lou was gone from the game. With Boyer playing Brock on a regular basis, he performed like a kid again.

Seeing a film of Brock's 3,000th base hit on television gave me a wonderful feeling, the same feeling I'd had in 1961 when I watched him knock the ball through the pitcher's mound and out into center field. I would have preferred that Brock had been able to accumulate his three grand plus safeties and 900 plus stolen bases as a Cub, but at the end it really didn't matter; Lou Brock, like Willie Mays, had been a gift to baseball.

FIFTY

On a September afternoon in 1978 I went to a ball game at Wrigley Field for the first time in nearly fifteen years. It was a strange, almost surreal experience for me. The fans looked the same, as did the field, especially Mrs. Wrigley's ivy. The only immediate difference I could discern was the wire basket-like extension that ran the length of the bleachers which had been constructed several years before in order to prevent fans from interfering with the ball. Pat Peiper, the field announcer, who had been on the job since the park opened in 1916, was still alive then and still working. "Have your pencil . . . and scorecard ready . . . for the correct lineups . . . for today's ball game," he barked, and I felt as if I'd never left. St. Louis beat the Cubs that day 4 to 1 and nobody could convince me afterward that anything had changed.

I was in Chicago only briefly on that trip, and I determined to come back and spend a week or two sitting again in the bleachers every day as Big Steve and I had done for fifty games a year during the '50s and early '60s. The opportunity did not present itself until the summer of 1980. I checked the schedule in advance and decided on an early August home stand that included Pittsburgh, Montreal, and Philadelphia, with Dave Kingman T-shirt Day planned as a special event for a Thursday afternoon game against the Pirates, baseball's champions of 1979.

I looked upon my return as a kind of religious reprise. I'd be doing it for Big Steve as well as myself; and for Don Landrum and Andy Pafko and Bobby Thomson; for Lou Brock, Hank

Aaron, Roberto Clemente, and Willie Mays; for all of those now fabled boys and men I'd never met yet knew so intimately. It didn't matter where they were, what they were, or even if they were today. They were yesterday, a day that for me and Big Steve and countless others had never ended.

The 1980 season, however, was another day, and by the looks of it, the Cubs were in big trouble. The headline for the Chicago Cub report in the June 21, 1980, issue of *The Sporting News* read: "Cubs in Crisis . . . Look for Shakeup." The Cubs were losing; their base running, fielding, and pitching had collapsed; Bruce Sutter was unhappy (the Jose Cardenal syndrome—but for the first time in his career his ERA was above 4.00); and on Friday the thirteenth of June, Dave Kingman went AWOL. The fans were reportedly restive, pitcher Willie Hernandez having drop-kicked his glove into the stands on May 31 in response to the booing. Nationally syndicated columnist Mike Royko wrote a piece about Hernandez slugging a spectator who'd gotten on his case; and infielder Steve Ontiveros, upset about losing his third-base job to Lenny Randle (the ex-Texas player who'd busted then Ranger manager Frank Lucchesi's jaw), quit the Cubs and signed a two-year contract with the Seibu team in Japan. I was prepared for the worst.

On July 2, the exact midpoint of the year, National Public Radio's "All Things Considered" news program broadcast an index of items by which one could be certain the year had achieved half-mast, one of the most memorable being the Chicago Cubs' marked movement toward their accustomed place in the National League standings: last.

PART 2

THE PAST SUSTAINED

Further in Summer than the Birds
Pathetic from the Grass
A minor Nation celebrates
Its unobtrusive Mass.

—EMILY DICKINSON

ONE

Throughout the 1970s I played on a variety of slow-pitch and fast-pitch softball teams, mostly in industrial leagues in Oakland, California. Slow-pitch I grew steadily to despise as being something quite apart from baseball. There were some fine players in those slow-pitch leagues, but any game that prohibited the stealing of bases and bunting and depended on a strike being called on a pitch that passed over the batter's head was certainly not hard ball and not for me. It differed, too, from the softball we'd played back in the old neighborhood because the size of the ball was twelve inches, not sixteen, and the fielders wore gloves, something that was forbidden in sixteen-inch, a handicap that added to the art. Everybody could hit in slow-pitch, the ball being lobbed in on a high arc, and while it was fun to run the bases again I found it a hard game to accept seriously.

The fast-pitch games were extremely tough and exciting, except when a pitcher was so dominant as to completely shut down the other team. It was baseball, though, even if the ball was still too large, and a marked contrast to slow-pitch. In the last couple of years of the decade, however, I turned my energies to basketball, it being a less formal sport when participated in on a playground level, and one that provided more exercise. As a friend commented, "You have to be *in* shape to play baseball; you can't play yourself into shape on a ball field. Basketball will get you into shape in a hurry; or kill you in the process."

I found that by playing basketball regularly I stayed in good shape and didn't have to deal with the social organization that goes with baseball. Pick-up b-ball games at the park did not require much socializing, just getting the ball in the hoop. It also eliminated having to deal with those individuals who had not made the grade at baseball earlier in life, when it had counted. For some reason I encountered this much more often on the baseball field than on the basketball court; I suppose it's because baseball *looks* so easy that anyone can imagine himself a star. The softball leagues—slow-pitch, not modified or fast-pitch—were full of thirty-to-forty-year-old self-proclaimed All-Stars who drove themselves as relentlessly as any twelve-year-old. These people were too serious for me, and I gladly left them to their fantasy.

I thought about this while listening to the 1980 All-Star game on the radio a few weeks before leaving for Chicago. I was glad I'd played baseball when I had and as well as I had. I would have liked to have been able to play even better (who wouldn't?), but I was satisfied with the way things had worked out for me. My son, at five years old, showed signs of becoming a genuine left-handed power hitter. I was encouraging but—visions of *Fear Strikes Out*, Jimmy Piersall's boyhood horror story—I didn't intend to push him into athletics of any kind. Although, I couldn't help but remind myself, a big, strong left-handed hitter with power who threw righty (as did my son) would be a much sought-after item by any big league club. But time would tell.

In the All-Star Game, which was being played in Los Angeles for the first time since 1958, the National League came back from a two-run deficit to defeat the American League, as could have been (and was) expected. Bruce Sutter, who pitched two no-hit innings to get the save, was the only Cub to appear in the game. The next day my press credentials arrived and I was getting anxious to go to Chicago, though news from my native habitat was less than encouraging.

Disgusted by the Cubs' "woeful performance," reported the *San Francisco Chronicle* Sporting Green on Wednesday, July 16 (the baby Bruins were already in last place in the National League East, 11 games behind division leader Montreal and sinking fast),

Chicago talk-show host Chuck Swirsky had begun promoting a "Snub the Cubs" day, urging fans to boycott the August 29 game against Houston at Wrigley Field. "We want to protest the amazing ineptitude of both the players and the front office," he said.

Not all Cub partisans felt the same as Mr. Swirsky, however. According to an item in *The Sporting News* of July 26, one Maniford "Hack" Harper, of Washburn, Illinois, a loyal Cub fan for fifty-four of his sixty-five years, made provisions with a mortician that upon his death Mr. Harper would be buried in a Chicago Cub uniform. "I'm going to be buried in the uniform because baseball is all I can think about," Harper said. "It's my life. I don't care about cars or anything else, and I never have."

Harper had been stricken with polio as an eleven-year-old and had been visited in the hospital by slugger Hack Wilson and other Cub players. Wilson had tapped Harper on the shoulder and encouraged him to "stick it out, kid. Someday you'll be able to walk." Ever since then Harper's friends had called him by the home run champion's name.

At thirteen, Hack Harper had the word CUBS tattooed on his left forearm in inch-high letters. Upon his high school graduation, Harper took a twenty-five-dollar gift and traveled the 125 miles to Chicago, where he watched the Cubs play for a week. Hack claimed to have attended more than 1,500 Cub games and collected 187 foul balls, all of which he'd had autographed and which he kept in a safety deposit box. For seven years straight he'd traveled to Arizona and purchased the first spring training ticket of the season.

"They're my whole life," said Harper. "Without the Cubs I would be crazy."

On Friday, July 25, Cub General Manager Bob Kennedy fired manager Preston Gomez, whom, three months before, Kennedy had called "one of the smartest men in baseball," and replaced him with ex-Cub player and two-time Cub coach Joey Amalfitano. Cy Young Award–winning relief pitcher Bruce Sutter said he was pleased for Amalfitano but upset for Gomez, that the Cubs' poor performance was Kennedy's fault for not "getting us more players. Preston did a good job with what we have. I don't think any manager we get would make much difference," Sutter said. "We've played terrible."

For his part, the deposed Preston Gomez admitted after his dismissal that he had known he was involved in a losing cause as early as the second day of spring training. There were "more unhappy players than I've ever seen on any team," Gomez said, and "no kind of an organization. I asked myself, 'What in the hell are you doing here?' "

Ed Sudol, a highly respected National League umpire for twenty years (1957–77), put Gomez "at the top of the list" of managers he'd observed. "He was a very good manager," said Sudol, "and to go along with his ability was a temperament that made him particularly outstanding to work with. . . . He was, in a word, a gentleman."

Bruce Sutter was joined in his assessment by a fan from Scranton, Pennsylvania, who wrote to *The Sporting News:* "If the Ayatollah Khomeini owned the Chicago Cubs, there would be executions after every game."

TWO

"Maybe that's what happens when you haven't won a pennant for thirty-five years," Cub outfielder Scot Thompson said on Dave Kingman T-shirt Day at Wrigley Field. "If I'd started watching the Cubs as a boy and ended up empty with my grandchildren sitting beside me, I might boo Kingman myself."

It was a ninety-eight-degree August 7 in Chicago and the Cubs' big slugger had been out with a shoulder injury since the All-Star break; had, in fact, played in but 47 of the Cubs' 104 games. The Cubs had just lost their third game in a row, 11 to 3, to Pittsburgh, and the 28,364 fans (on a Thursday afternoon!) reacted with uncustomary venom to every mention of Kingman's name.

Both fans and local scribes considered Dave a malingerer, feeling that even though he might not be in a playable condition, the least he could do would be to provide the team support by lending his presence in the dugout during games, an activity he openly disdained.* One teammate termed Kingman's noninvolvement as "sick." Sportswriters from the Chicago area dailies were less than charitable toward Dave, an attitude derived from an episode earlier in the season when Kingman had dumped a

---

*In January of 1981 Chicago radio station WLS polled its listeners to determine who the fans considered the city's biggest sports flop of 1980. Ninety percent of the votes went to Dave Kingman.

bucket of ice over a reporter's head. But it certainly wasn't only the big guy's fault that the Cubs had slid deeper into the cellar, 16 games off the pace set by the incoming Montreal Expos.

The fans I spoke to expressed their displeasure with the Cub front office, believing that management refused to spend the money necessary to acquire free agents like Reggie Jackson. Kingman, one fan opined, was a dud who would be—and apparently was—unhappy anywhere he landed. On the other hand, one fan—who had driven 180 miles from Fort Wayne, Indiana (Cincinnati Reds country, he called it), to see the Cubs play Pittsburgh—would be happy to see Reggie in Wrigley's right field. "Jackson's worth it," he said. "He puts out, plays hurt. I wouldn't mind seeing *him* get two or three million."

In general, however, the working-class Cub fans resented the players' astronomical salaries. This paradox concerning player-management financial relations was a conundrum most fans were hard put to reconcile satisfactorily. The point seemed to me to be that the basic nature of professional baseball had changed. No longer was it just a game, it was "entertainment," on a par with Elvis at the MGM Grand in Vegas.

Reporters who followed the team said the Cub players were unhappy and wanted out. Outfielder Jerry Martin, who by the end of the first week in August had already exceeded his previous best year's homer output with 20, turned down a generous six-figure three-year pact in order to place himself in the free market. This 1980 Cub squad was a strange assortment of odds and ends, only a few of whom—Bill Buckner (the steadiest Cub, hitting well over .300), Bruce Sutter,* Rick Reuschel, rookie Jesus Figueroa** (oodles of potential), Ivan DeJesus (of whom Bob Kennedy

---

*Sutter was traded to the St. Louis Cardinals on December 9, 1980. "I just couldn't see the Cubs [winning the pennant] during my career," he said. "I just don't see any chance of the Cubs becoming a winner. There's not much in their minor league system and it's pretty obvious we didn't have enough talent up here. It seems like the minute you become good around here and they have to pay you for being good, then they get rid of you because they don't want to pay you. You just can't operate that way, I don't think. Baseball is a big business now."

**Figueroa was traded to the Giants during the off-season.

Billy Williams (Wide World)

said, "He's like Minnie Minoso. He gives you that steady game, day in and day out, year after year"), maybe Martin,* appeared worth including in the building of a contender.

---

*Martin also went to the Giants following the 1980 campaign.

167

The Cub management's policy of not putting up with malcontents, of making little or no effort to appease those athletes who for one reason or another appeared disaffected (viz. Cardenal, etc.), had not changed, leading most observers to suspect that Mr. Kingman's days as a Cub were numbered. G.M. Bob Kennedy admitted that he had attempted to trade Big Dave, despite his spectacular '79 season, in May to Pittsburgh for pitcher Bert Blyleven and infielder Dale Berra, but the Pirates turned him down.*

In other words, the view from the stands or press box at Wrigley Field in the first season of the Orwellian era, the thirty-fifth since a championship flag of any kind flew above the ivy, was much the same as it had been when I was a boy. Scot Thompson's assessment of the situation notwithstanding, this was—almost incredibly—yet another version of mediocrity, or less.

Still the fans come, cloaking their disappointment with a kind of indefatigably optimistic pleasure not often seen in this most modern era: disco music on the loudspeaker, gold chains strung round nearly every neck (even coach Billy Williams's, his handsome, graying eminence magically notable amongst the mostly anonymous new Cub faces, his sinewy, veined forearms appearing quite capable of stinging line drives over the right-field catwalk).

Dave Kingman T-shirt Day was notable, too, for the performance of Pirate pitcher Eddie Solomon, a former Cub, who in 1975 had been considered, according to *Sun-Times* writer Joe Goddard, "incorrigible" by Cub management, and was dealt during that season to the Atlanta Braves. Solomon, however, had refused to go quietly, showing up in the bullpen in his Chicago uniform twenty-four hours after the deal was announced, refusing to leave. Cub radio broadcaster Lou Boudreau defined Solomon's actions of that period as those of "a troubled young man," a designation not contradicted by a spring training incident in

---

*On the last day of February 1981, Kingman was returned to the Mets for outfielder Steve Henderson.

Palm Beach in 1980 in which Solomon was detained by authorities for brandishing a gun in a restaurant.

The pitcher looked anything but troubled in his stint versus the Cubs during the Pirates' usual backstretch drive toward the flag, hurling a complete-game eight-hitter to raise his won-lost record to 6 and 3 and elevate Pittsburgh to within a game and a half of Montreal. "This has to rank as one of my top games," said Solomon, "but it made no difference [that] it was against the Cubs."

"The Cubs give up on young players too soon," said a fan in the right-field bleachers, still the easiest spot in the park in which to place a bet. "They [the front office] want results right away, and when they don't get it, don't give the young guys enough time to develop properly, poof! they're gone. You remember Lou Brock," he said to me, "don't you?"

THREE

The plant itself, Wrigley Field, was as beautiful in 1980 as it had been when I first entered it in 1952. The Baby Ruth candy bar sign that had been on the roof of a building beyond the right-field fence was gone, however. That sign had been a favorite symbol of mine, since as a young fan I had imagined its presence was due not to the advertisement of a candy bar but as a marker for a home run Babe Ruth had deposited in that spot at a moment in the mythological baseball past. Elmer, Wrigley's ancient press box custodian, told me it had been replaced by another sign sometime during Durocher's reign, and the roof now stood bare. (The Baby Ruth candy bar, by the way, as pointed out to me by the "Baseball Professor," Jim "The Jet" Carothers, was not named after the Yankee slugger but a different bambino altogether, President Grover Cleveland's daughter.)

The Babe, of course, had hit his legendary called-shot homer —when he supposedly pointed to the bleachers before swatting one into the seats—in Wrigley Field during the 1932 World Series. Since the veracity of that epic clout was dubious, the Baby Ruth sign for me had always evidenced more realistically the Babe's presence, even in Chicago, as Lord of Baseball. Not having that tangible evidence in view, however self-created a delusion, was somewhat of a disappointment.

Chicago, however, still impressed me as a tough place, even a mean one. A high-steel worker friend of mine in San Francisco had had a brother shot and killed by a robber in a bar on the

South Side of Chicago only a short time ago, something that could, of course, happen anywhere, but always seems more prevalent in Chicago. I was back in the biggest small town in the world, and it was difficult for me to believe that I, along with Big Steve and Magic Frank, had once considered it the greatest city of all. That youthful opinion, however, was easy to explain as a kind of naïve, parochial pride, being that it was then the only city any of us really knew.

A tour of the old neighborhood revealed the streets and houses to be relatively unchanged, though Green Briar Park had been altered to accommodate a new small-children's play area and two all-screen baseball backstops had replaced the original wooden ones. Also, the former local supermarket had been transformed into the Croatian Cultural Center of Chicago. Driving around town with Magic Frank, who had moved to a northwest suburb in order to be nearer the airport—his job required extensive travel—I was pleased to discover that good AM radio stations still existed. We cruised along listening to Purvis Spann, the longtime WVON soul music deejay, now on WXOL, play tracks by B. B. King, Aretha Franklin, Ray Charles, and the Mighty Clouds of Joy, reminding me of "Daddio's Jazz Patio" with Daddio Daylie on WAAF, and Big Bill Hill's "Shoppingbag Show" on WOPA, the finest blues station of its day. As teenagers, Magic and I had been WOPA devotees of the loyalest order. Big Bill would play records he liked over and over again, especially ones by Eddie Boyd, while taking refreshment from his shopping bag, the clink of glass clearly audible in the background. I remembered, too, that Jimmy Yancey, the legendary blues and boogie-woogie piano player, had been a groundskeeper at Comiskey Park, home of the White Sox, until his death in 1951. I doubt that the Sox organization knew they had such a man of distinction rolling out the tarp over the infield for them on rainy days.

At our old grammar school, Frank recalled how his oldest brother, Jerry, had hit a softball onto the roof from the farthest playground diamond, a feat that still had apparently not been duplicated. At the high school he reminded me of the time in 1963 when blacks picketed the school in protest over racial imbalance at that institution, an absolutely legitimate cavil of that period but one which, as I remember it, all but completely mystified the students. Nobody could understand why *anyone* would want to go to school there.

Frank had calmed down considerably since our grammar school days when he used to post daily on his locker a list of names of those individuals he would fight after school. Sometimes he put people on the list who didn't want to fight, and if they didn't show up it just worked to Frank's credit. He told me the reason he'd fought so much in those days was that his father had died and he hadn't had the proper guidance a father might have provided.

"What about your older brothers?" I asked him. "Woody and Jerry—didn't they help you out?"

"Yeah," said Frank, and laughed. "Remember the time Woody broke the leg of that kid from St. Tim's who hit me over the head with the bat?"

The only real shock was that the Villa Girgenti restaurant and Bebop's Pool Hall had been torn down. No vestiges of the buildings remained. I reminded Frank about the time we were at the Villa and he went over to a 400-pound guy who was eating two large pizzas at one time and asked admiringly if he could watch. "Yeah, losing the Villa was a real tragedy," said Magic Frank. "It's hard to believe it's gone. I consider it to have been one of the really great all-around restaurants of all time."

Frank asked if I remembered Chicken Charlie, a wizened old black guy who used to appear irregularly in front of Wrigley Field with a live chicken on his head. He'd ride around Chicago on buses, though drivers often gave him a hard time about the chicken. He'd stand in front of the park, open a bottle of beer, and pour a little for the chicken into the bottle cap, chattering away between toothless gums animatedly and indecipherably— to the human ear; maybe the chicken understood what he was saying—while playing with and showing off to the kids the numerous items strung around his neck: a baby doll, a telephone (into which he'd carry on lengthy imaginary conversations), whistles, and other paraphernalia. But I think that Chicken Charlie was a White Sox fan because I once saw him on Maxwell Street collecting change in a Sox cap. The chicken's only passion seemed to be for beer.

FOUR

The afternoon following the Dave Kingman T-shirt Day debacle, prior to the commencement of the regularly scheduled contest, the Cubs and Expos resumed play in the eleventh inning of a tie game that had been suspended earlier in the year. In the bottom of the fifteenth inning Cub first baseman Cliff Johnson (who a year before had put his Yankee teammate Goose Gossage out for much of the season with a broken thumb, the result of a locker room tête-à-tête), who was not even a member of the Cubs when the game had started—having since been acquired from Cleveland—socked a grand-slam home run to win the game.

This victory posed an interesting problem for statisticians: should the win be credited to the managerial record of Preston Gomez, who had been the Cub skipper for the initial 10 innings, or to his replacement, Joey Amalfitano, who was there at the end? The press box conjecture concerning this question concluded with the awarding of the triumph to Amalfitano, with, however (following the precedent set in 1961 by Roger Maris' 61 home runs in 162 games, as opposed to Ruth's record of 60 in a 154-game schedule), an asterisk.*

The graffiti on the wall of the pissoir adjacent to the press box at Wrigley Field is a monument to Cub history and will, hopefully, be preserved and reconstructed one day in the Hall of

---

*"Has anyone ever actually *seen* that asterisk?" joked one wiseguy journalist.

Fame at Cooperstown. Among the names scratched on the cracked yellow plaster are those of Ed Winceniak, Jack Littrell, Woody English, Boots Day, Cuno Barragan, Don Landrum(!), Norm Gigon, and Bob Buhl; scrawled just above and to the right of the urinal is the desperate plea: *Moose must go!*

Seeing Pirate second baseman Phil Garner lose a pop fly in short right, Wrigley's deadly late-afternoon sun field, I recalled a game in the late '50s against the Braves when Hank Aaron missed two fly balls in a row in the bottom of the eighth or ninth inning to give the Cubs the win. Aaron was a very reliable outfielder but was no match for the sun that day, letting each ball fall untouched on the grass nearby. For different reasons, like that game I attended at Candlestick Park a dozen years before, Wrigley Field was full of ghosts for me. In comparison to the present-day Cub team, the ghosts were far more pleasing to watch.

That evening I drove by the now-abandoned storefront on Western Avenue that had been Friedman's Delicatessen while I was growing up. Big Steve and I had hung out there regularly, going late at night to get the early edition of the next-day's *Sun-Times* to check the sports results from the East Coast. Friedman's had been the neighborhood's unofficial bookie joint, always full of guys named Louie who wore little checkered hats with a feather in the band. Whenever the pay phone in the rear rang all of the Louies made for it like Lou Brock stealing second. The owner finally had the phone taken out. Years later, during the abortive attempt to establish off-track betting in Chicago, in a perfectly appropriate bit of planning, Friedman's had been designated as one of the outlets.

FIVE

Big Steve came in from New York for the Montreal series and we had a couple of serious discussions concerning the Cubs' continuing mediocrity. Steve's main contention as to why the Cubs hadn't been able to compete successfully since 1945 was that the team was the play toy of a rich man, P. K. Wrigley, who enjoyed being an owner only so long as he didn't have to take the whole thing too seriously. Steve reminded me of a radio advertisement for the Cubs that ran for years, something like: "Come on out and have a picnic at Wrigley Field, enjoy the fresh air, green grass, and see a major league ball game besides."

In the '50s the Cubs drew poorly, as did many other major league franchises. Attendance picked up again in the mid-'60s when baseball experienced a rebirth of fan interest. Virtually all of the Cub games, home and away, were televised, and eventually this practice served to provide the same kind of free advertising having records played on the radio did for record companies. In the early days of radio, record companies were reluctant to allow their discs to be played on the air for fear that nobody would buy them if they could hear them for free. The opposite, of course, turned out to be the case—when people heard a tune they liked on the radio they were inspired to go out and buy it. The same principle provided the Cubs a fan identification that eventually helped to benefit them substantially at the gate despite the lack of a winning team.

Wrigley Field itself was a draw, and not just for its unique beauty. Because of its small size and winds favorable to the hitters, fans could usually count on seeing a competitive game with lots of runs being scored. Fenway Park in Boston offered the same thing, drawing consistently good crowds despite the Red Sox' perennial also-ran status.

The Cubs' failure in post–World War II times is not the product of any one thing. The Wrigley ownership attitude toward the team as a pleasant hobby is perhaps the most important; the Yankees of the 1970s and '80s win because owner George Steinbrenner is *determined* to do so. Phil Wrigley's "plantation" attitude, as Big Steve called it, of keeping around those athletes whom he deemed good fellows, often past the point of valuable production, contributed significantly to the team's downfall. (Ernie Banks, for all of his greatness, stayed at shortstop past his ability to handle the position, with Phil Wrigley's blessing.)

Wrigley's hiring of his former pet players, such as Stan Hack and Bob Scheffing, to manage the club, prompted author-pitcher Jim Brosnan to comment: "Wrigley was perfectly willing to hire his old athletes instead of bright, hardworking people." Perhaps the most outrageous of all of P.K.'s moves was to award, in 1975, Salty Saltwell, who had previously been in charge of hot dog sales, the job of general manager. Salty lasted only one year in the front office.

Those who rocked the boat, or threatened to, were most often quickly dispatched elsewhere. The mark of the Wrigley organization has been to take the easy way out, to opt for the immediate result, the quick fix, rather than attempt to build a team for the future. To be sure, a certain amount of bad luck has entered into it, such as second baseman Ken Hubbs's premature death; but there was the poor judgment that insisted on using Jim Brewer as a starting pitcher rather than as the brilliant reliever he proved he could be with the Dodgers; the acquisition of Ralph Kiner and Frank Thomas, players who were past their prime, who could still give the crowd an occasional thrill with the long ball but weren't about to be included in a rebuilding effort; the mishandling of Adolpho Phillips; and the Brock-for-Broglio disaster.

The bottom line for all of this is attitude: when the players feel that management, for whatever reason, places winning at a priority level other than foremost, they tend to play at that level or below. It is no accident that the Cubs have not won even so much as a division title since a one-armed player patrolled the outfield for the St. Louis Browns. Just as at the roulette wheel there is no assurance that the ball will land on red following any number of consecutive shows of black, so there is no reason, despite the so-called law of averages, to believe that the Cubs will win a pennant anytime soon. Just fielding a team is not enough. A change in the philosophy of ownership, the fortuitous acquisition of three or four key players all at once: these might bring about the adjustments necessary to the establishment of a winning team.

"You keep thinking things are going to change around here," said Cub pitcher Bruce Sutter, "and they don't." Even Bill Buckner, battling for the National League batting title* and playing a hustling left field despite two sore ankles, could not help being down. "It sounds terrible," Buckner said as the season moved into its final stage, "but I just can't stand the thought of another month of this. At least in the past here, there has been something to drive for. If we're in fourth, we try for third. But now, let's face it, there's nothing. Nothing. I've never been this depressed ever in baseball."

When other Cub players began to talk about playing a "spoiler" role in important season's-end series against Pittsburgh, Montreal, and Philadelphia, pitcher Rick Reuschel snapped angrily, "Spoilers! The only thing that we're going to spoil, we've already spoiled. And that's our season."

The Wrigley Company accountants couldn't have been too pleased with the sporting side of the organization, either; according to *Crain's Chicago Business* the Cubs had lost $1.7 million for the nine-month period ending in July 1980.

---

*Buckner won the National League batting crown in 1980 with an average of .324.

SIX

"Cub Notes" in the *Chicago Sun-Times* of August 9, 1980, quoted General Manager Bob Kennedy concerning a six-hour organizational meeting presided over by Cub owner Bill Wrigley, son of P.K., held in Kennedy's Wrigley Field office. "We had everyone there," Kennedy said. "Our top scouts, our minor league managers, and Vedie Himsl [one of the original rotating coaches of the '60s] and Carol Davis, who run the farm system. Later, we were joined by [Cub field manager] Joe Amalfitano and his coaches. We reviewed the players we have and what positions we might have to fill next season."

Never once when I was a boy did I hear or read of old P.K. participating in such a meeting, leading one to believe that perhaps the times *are* finally changing, and that under the more actively participatory ownership of Bill Wrigley—who inherited the team upon his father's death in 1977—optimism may not be unfounded.

Despite the drought of the last thirty-five years, the Cubs' 16 pennants place them second only to the Giants' 18 in National League history. They hold the all-time major league record for wins in a season, 116, and winning percentage, .763, both accomplished in 1906. They have won more games than any other team in major league history. And Cub fans still stand during the seventh-inning stretch and sing "Take Me Out to the Ball Game." Chicago Cub fans are knowledgeable, too, unlike those on the West Coast—they know who the players are, know the rules of the game, and respond appropriately to the action. This, plus their obvious loyalty, certainly entitles them to something better. "It's a shame," said former Cub pitcher Steve Stone, another outstanding hurler the Cubs gave up on too soon, "because Chicago is the best baseball city in the country, with the best and most tolerant fans. But the Cubs never fostered a feeling of pride in their players, never gave you the feeling you were something special."

Leo Durocher brought the Cubs up from their twenty-consecutive-season residence (1947–66)—a major league record—in the second division, but after his departure in 1972 they have not again been above .500. "It took the White Sox forty years to win their last pennant," said Phil Wrigley in 1965. "At that rate, we've still got twenty years to go." Now, in 1980, assured of being the only National League team to go thirty-five years without a league championship, according to Wrigley's rival timetable there are only five years left in which to at least match the Sox record. Things being what they are, it would take a fanatic or a fool to bet on the Cubs' chances of accomplishing even that.

During the game against Montreal on August 9 a plane flew over Wrigley Field trailing a banner that read: "Bill, Karen & Lee Think The Cubs Stink." They weren't alone in their thinking. A *Chicago Tribune* poll showed that 89 percent of its readers who responded felt that William Wrigley should sell the team; the same poll revealed an 84 percent negative response to the efforts of General Manager Bob Kennedy. Wrigley's answer was that he had no intention to sell. Bob Kennedy, who in his four years as G.M. had been hamstrung by a lower budget than that accorded most other teams, was criticized by fans as being a poor trader and a company man. "The fans are entitled to their opinions," he said.

One fan's opinion, expressed in an open letter, while a trifle convoluted, must have left Kennedy wondering whether there couldn't be an easier way for him to make a living. "The Cub fans who have been writing to *The Sporting News* complaining about General Manager Bob Kennedy should forget about it," wrote Frank Fisher of Chicago. "William Wrigley will never fire the ultra-inept Kennedy as Kennedy's salary is doubtlessly being paid by other teams. And why not? Kennedy is a good instrument for opposing general managers who reap their rewards in the form of good players received from the Cubs in exchange for their culls."

According to a statement he gave to the *New York Times*, owner Bill Wrigley could not even keep track of what those deals actually were. He told the *Times* that he considered the 1979 Bobby Murcer trade "a great deal" because it brought pitcher Dick Tidrow to the Cubs. Murcer, as Bob Kennedy no doubt could have reminded his boss, went to the Yankees for money and a minor league pitcher. Tidrow had come to Chicago for hurler Ray Burris a month earlier.

SEVEN

I can't help but feel that the period during which the Cubs were perennial second-division dwellers, the mid-'40s through the early '60s, was perhaps the last era in which major league baseball was and forever will be truly great. There were fewer teams, the minor leagues were still extensive, and a majority of the best professional athletes in the United States and neighboring Latin countries chose to play baseball rather than football, basketball, or soccer.

Beginning in the late '40s, black athletes went into major league baseball because of the unwritten quota systems imposed by professional football and basketball teams, and so baseball fans were privileged to witness the performances of Willie Mays, Jackie Robinson, Frank Robinson, Roy Campanella, Roberto Clemente, Ernie Banks, Billy Williams, Lou Brock, Hank Aaron, and so many others. Along with white stars such as Stan Musial, Ted Williams, Mickey Mantle, Al Kaline, Duke Snider, Warren Spahn, Brooks Robinson, et al., that twenty-year stretch constituted an era of individual excellence baseball fans are unlikely to see again.

The best athletes of today are spread across too many sports ever to have the concentration of top-level performers baseball used to enjoy. Because of that, because of the diminution of the minor leagues and the continuing expansion of major league franchises thinning out the talent, too many of what were formerly considered second- or third-rate players populate the game. There never has been a time in which there were enough good pitchers to make up the entire staffs of each major league team, and since the first American League expansion in 1961 and National League expansion in 1962 the pitching ranks have suffered severely. Sparky Anderson, former Cincinnati and current Detroit manager, recently asserted that pitching talent in the bigs may be thinner now than ever: "There's just no way to supply twenty-six teams," said Anderson. "Even the clubs with good pitching have only six or seven reliable arms."

As baseball has moved into a generally more mediocre phase, also-rans such as the Cubs, Cleveland Indians, and White Sox have become even less strong, while franchises able and willing to spend the most money—the Yankees, above all—have more firmly established their dominance. "I have outlived my usefulness," said Phil Wrigley in 1977, not long before he died. "Everything has changed." Everything, it must be added, but the Cubs.

EIGHT

I went back to the old neighborhood one more time on the day before I was to leave Chicago. I was on my way to Wrigley Field for a Monday game with the Phillies when I decided to drive by my old house again. I parked the car and walked down the narrow gangway to the backyard; I wanted to see the garage wall I had spent so many hours bouncing a ball against. Coming into the yard from the alleyway entrance at the same time was a woman I recognized instantly, the mother of my childhood friend and next-door neighbor Johnny McLaughlin.

Mrs. McLaughlin knew me right away, and we both laughed as we shook hands and asked what the other was doing there. We hadn't seen one another for sixteen years. She told me I looked the same and I told her she did, too, only smaller, like the yard and the buildings. When you're a kid people and things look so big to you, and they stay that way in your memory. I explained that I was in town doing research for a book and she told me she and her husband, Frank, who had been a doorman at the Drake Hotel for forty years, still lived next door. Her son Johnny was an electrical engineer, was married, had kids, lived in a suburb.

The neighborhood, Mrs. McLaughlin said, had deteriorated, but not too badly. Even if it got worse she wouldn't move, she said. "Where would we go?" St. Timothy's was doing better than ever; this was Chicago, after all, the Catholic community was still strong. (In addition to the considerable Irish-Catholic citizenry, outside of Warsaw the city with the largest Polish population is

Chicago, better than 90 percent of whom are Catholic.) I reminded her of the hours I spent sitting on her back porch after dinner waiting for Johnny and his younger brother, Billy, to finish saying the rosary with the family before they could come out to play. She told me another neighborhood boyhood buddy, Johnny Clements, had become a priest. We went over to her house and I said hello to Mr. McLaughlin, who, I was glad to see, was still in good shape. I told him that he looked shorter than I remembered him being and he laughed. "You haven't lost your accent, though," I said, referring to his still-heavy brogue. Mr. and Mrs. McLaughlin used to speak to each other in Gaelic whenever they didn't want the kids to know what they were talking about.

We exchanged family news, and after a while I said I had to go, that I was on my way to Wrigley Field. "Still a Cub fan, are ya?" said Mr. McLaughlin. "I'm afraid so," I said. "Ah, you're a nice fella, Barry," he said, "what do ya want to go and give yourself all that pain for?"

At the ball park the Phillies scored one in the first on a walk, a stolen base on which there was a bad throw by the Cub catcher enabling the runner to go to third, and a sacrifice fly. Philadelphia scored another in the second and one in the third on third baseman Mike Schmidt's 28th home run of the year, the 26th homer of his career in Wrigley Field. In between the second and third innings there was a rain delay of one hour and fifty-two minutes, during which Elmer, the press box custodian, remarked, "They should have called this game at one-thirty [starting time] for lack of interest."

After Schmidt's homer the sun came out and I broke my oft-made promise to myself about never leaving a ball game before it was over. It didn't matter whether the Cubs won or lost this one; they weren't going anywhere, hadn't been anywhere since the year before before I could walk, and they didn't really seem to care. I hadn't lived in Chicago for half of my life. The logical thing to do, it occurred to me as I walked west on Addison Street, away from Wrigley Field, would be to reconsider my allegiance.

NINE

As I headed west on Irving Park Road toward the tollway that would take me out to Magic Frank's house, it began to sprinkle again, and I recalled the time my mother and I drove from Chicago to Jackson, Mississippi, in a steady rainstorm in her boyfriend Irwin's Jaguar sedan. Irwin owned a girdle factory on Clinton Street and we stopped there on our way out of Chicago. I waited in the car while my mother went into the factory to talk to Irwin, who was going to fly in an airplane down to Jackson and meet us there.

I was six years old and was playing with some toy soldiers on the backseat of the Jaguar, waiting for my mother, when a dark-faced man with a mustache stuck his head in the window on the passenger side and smiled. "Hey, muchacho," he said, "this your car?" I didn't say anything. "What do you think, we sell this car, make big money," he said, spreading his arms wide. He had a handsome Latin smile with gold teeth in it. "How about it?" he asked.

"It's not my mother's car," I said. "She'll be back in a minute from the girdle factory."

"I was ballplayer once," said the man. "In my country. I had big car like this. I was big hero." He spread his arms wide again.

I turned my attention back to my soldiers, and when I looked up the man was gone. My mother came back to the car and I told her a man had wanted to sell it. "This is a bad neighborhood," she said. "You shouldn't talk to strange men."

"He said he was a ballplayer," I told her.

"Even so," she said.

We drove straight through to Tennessee and got a room in a hilltop motel. In the middle of the night I heard a scream and woke up. My mother was in the bathroom beating black bugs with her slipper. "We're leaving," she said. "Get dressed."

It was about three or four o'clock in the morning, but my mother woke up the man in the motel office and told him she was going. "There are roaches in that room," she said. "Thousands of them."

"Yes, ma'am," he said.

It was raining hard when we arrived in Jackson. Irwin had reserved a room for us in a hotel there and my mother and I took baths and went to bed even though it was daytime. "At least it's clean," she said.

We met Irwin that night for dinner. I was wearing my blue Cub cap with the red *C* on it. "Down here that stands for Cracker," he said.

Irwin told us he was going to build a girdle factory in Mississippi. He asked us if we wanted to drive out the next day to see where it was going to be and my mother said no, we were flying back to Chicago in the morning.

After breakfast we took a taxi to the airfield. It was still pouring when the plane took off.

TEN
Extra Inning

On my way back to the West Coast I stopped in Kansas City for ribs and to visit my old friend Jim Carothers. He and his seventeen-year-old son Mike picked me up at the airport, and after eating we went to the ball park to watch the Royals, who were leading the American League West by 13 games, play Baltimore, who were 2½ behind the Yankees in the East.

It was a great game, with the brilliant Kansas City third baseman George Brett, who was hitting an astounding .389 ("The only way to pitch him," said Yankee pitcher Rudy May, "is way inside, so you force him to pull the ball. That way, the line drive won't hit you"), battling Oriole left-hander Scott McGregor, fouling off six pitches in the process, and belting a triple to tie the game in the fifth. Brett also made a marvelous stab of a shot hit to his left to start a double play that second baseman Frank White turned superbly, making an extended pirouette in order to relay the ball perfectly to first. Kansas City left fielder Willie Wilson ran down a monster rip in the alley, making a sure triple into a third out; and old-timer Mark Belanger, the Baltimore shortstop, scooped up rocket after rocket off the blemish-free carpet like a Hoover. The Royals won the game in the bottom of the ninth on a bases-loaded walk off a 3 and 2 count that followed an intentional pass to Brett, and the full house went home happy.

The game "cleaned out [my] pipes," as Jim put it. It was wonderful, following a week or so of indifferent, so-so baseball in Chicago, to watch such a crisp performance. Out of habit I

George Brett (Photo by Leonard Kamsler from The Art of Hitting .300 *by Charley Lau with Alfred Glossbrenner)*

kept checking the scoreboard for news of the Cub game, but the Royals and Orioles made me feel positive again. It was to the sport itself, baseball, that I owed my allegiance, as well as to the Cubs. I could never deny my sentimental attachment to the Cubs; if they did all right that was a bonus, but the game played well was what it was really all about.

That night after the Kansas City–Baltimore game I dreamed that Chicken Charlie was doing his act in my old backyard. He poured some beer into the bottle cap for the chicken, took a big swig, and passed me the bottle. On the label was the Chicago Cub logo, a smiling little bear with the word CUBS on his belly. Chicken Charlie was grinning his toothless grin at me. I grinned back and finished off the beer.

APPENDIXES

MY ALL-TIME CHICAGO CUB TEAM 1952–PRESENT

This selection is composed only of players I have personally seen play who were with the Cubs either for the bulk of their career or who made significant contributions during their Cub tenure. The statistics that follow the names represent individual players' best season as a Cub.

Left Field: Billy Williams   1970   BA .322   HR 42   RBI 129
Center Field: George Altman   1961   BA .303   HR 27   RBI 96
Right Field: Hank Sauer   1954   BA .288   HR 41   RBI 103
Third Base: Ron Santo   1964   BA .313   HR 30   RBI 114   TRIPLES 13
Shortstop: Ivan DeJesus   1979   BA .283   R 92   RBI 52   SB 24
Second Base: Glenn Beckert   1971   BA .342
First Base: Ernie Banks   1958   BA .313   HR 47   RBI 129   TRIPLES 11
Catcher: Randy Hundley   1969   BA .255   HR 18   RBI 64
Left-handed Starting Pitcher: Dick Ellsworth   1963   W 22   L 10   ERA 2.11
Right-handed Starting Pitcher: Ferguson Jenkins   1971   W 24   L 13   ERA 2.77   CG 30   SO 263
Left-handed Relief Pitcher: Bill Henry   1959   G 65   W 9   L 8   ERA 2.68   SV 12
Right-handed Relief Pitcher: Bruce Sutter   1977   G 62   W 7   L 3   ERA 1.35   SV 31

Code: BA=batting average; HR=home runs; RBI=runs batted in; R=runs; SB =stolen bases; W=wins; L=losses; ERA=earned run average; CG=complete games; SO=strikeouts; SV=saves.

CUBS ALL-TIME TOP FIVE BATTERS SINCE 1900 (minimum 500 Games)

Games			Triples		
Banks	2,528		Schulte		117
Williams	2,213		Cavarretta		99
Santo	2,126		Tinker		93
Cavarretta	1,953		Banks		90
Hack	1,938		Williams		87

At Bats			Home Runs		
Banks	9,421		Banks		512
Williams	8,479		Williams		392
Santo	7,768		Santo		337
Hack	7,278		Hartnett		231
Cavarretta	6,592		Nicholson		205

Runs			RBI's		
Williams	1,306		Banks		1,636
Banks	1,305		Williams		1,354
Hack	1,239		Santo		1,290
Santo	1,109		Hartnett		1,153
Cavarretta	968		Cavarretta		896

Hits			Extra Base Hits		
Banks	2,583		Banks		1,009
Williams	2,510		Williams		881
Hack	2,193		Santo		756
Santo	2,171		Hartnett		686
Cavarretta	1,927		Cavarretta		532

Doubles			Career Batting Average		
Banks	407		Stephenson		.336
Williams	402		Cuyler		.325
Hartnett	391		Wilson		.322
Hack	363		Herman		.309
Santo	353		Demaree		.309

CUBS WORLD SERIES RECORDS

1906—Chicago (AL) beat CUBS, 4 games to 2.
1907—CUBS beat Detroit (AL), 4 games to 0.
1908—CUBS beat Detroit (AL), 4 games to 1.
1910—Philadelphia (AL) beat CUBS, 4 games to 1.
1918—Boston (AL) beat CUBS, 4 games to 2.
1929—Philadelphia (AL) beat CUBS, 4 games to 1.
1932—New York (AL) beat CUBS, 4 games to 0.
1935—Detroit (AL) beat CUBS, 4 games to 2.
1938—New York (AL) beat CUBS, 4 games to 0.
1945—Detroit (AL) beat CUBS, 4 games to 3.

Gold Glove Winners

1960	Ernie Banks, shortstop	1967	Randy Hundley, C;
1962	Ken Hubbs, 2B		Ron Santo, 3B
1964	Larry Jackson, P;	1968	Glenn Beckert, 2B;
	Ron Santo, 3B		Ron Santo, 3B
1965	Ron Santo, 3B	1969	Ernie Banks, 1B
1966	Ron Santo, 3B		Don Kessinger, SS
		1970	Don Kessinger, SS

CUBS TOP MARKS — SINCE 1900

SEASON BATTING

Games .... Ron Santo and Billy Williams (1965): 164
At Bats .... Billy Herman (1935): 666
Runs Scored .... Rogers Hornsby (1929): 156
Hits .... Rogers Hornsby (1929): 229
Singles .... Earl Adams (1927): 165
Doubles .... Billy Herman (1935, 1936): 57
Triples .... Frank Schulte (1911), Vic Saier (1913): 21
Home Runs .... Hack Wilson (1930): 56*
Total Bases .... Hack Wilson (1930): 423*
Runs Batted In .... Hack Wilson (1930): 190†
Extra Base Hits .... Hack Wilson (1930): 97*
Batting Average .... Rogers Hornsby (1929): .380
Slugging Average .... Hack Wilson (1930): .723
Grand Slam Home Runs .... Ernie Banks (1955): 5†
Home Runs — Rookie Season .... Billy Williams (1961): 25
Consecutive-Game Hitting Streak .... Ron Santo (1966): 28
Stolen Bases .... Frank Chance (1903): 67
Bases on Balls .... Jimmy Sheckard (1911): 147
Hit by Pitcher .... Adolfo Phillips (1966): 12

SEASON PITCHING

Game Won .... Mordecai Brown (1908): 29
Games Lost .... Tom Highes (1901), Dick Ellsworth (1966),
Bill Bonham (1974): 22
Complete
Games .... John Taylor (1903), Grover Alexander (1920): 33
Innings Pitched .... Grover Alexander (1920): 363
Percentage — 10 Games and Over .... Len Cole (1910) 20-4: .833
Percentage — Under 10 Games .... Ken Holtzman (1967) 9-0: 1000
Consecutive Games Won .... Ed Reulbach (1909): 14
Lowest Earned Run Average .... Mordecai Brown (1906): 1.04
Games Started .... Ferguson Jenkins (1969): 42
Games Finished .... Ted Abernathy (1965): 62
Most Appearances .... Ted Abernathy (1965): 84
Most Saves .... Bruce Sutter (1979): 37*
Strikeouts .... Ferguson Jenkins (1970): 274
Bases on Balls .... Sam Jones (1955): 185
Shutouts .... Mordecai Brown (1906, 1908), Orval Overall (1907,
1909), Grover Alexander (1919) and Bill Lee (1938): 9

CAREER BATTING

Games .... Ernie Banks: 2,528
Years .... Phil Cavarretta: 20
At Bats .... Ernie Banks: 9,421
Runs .... Billy Williams: 1,306
Hits .... Ernie Banks: 2,583
Doubles .... Ernie Banks: 407
Triples .... Frank Schulte: 117
Home Runs .... Ernie Banks: 512
Total Bases .... Ernie Banks: 4,706
Runs Batted In .... Ernie Banks: 1,636
Extra Base Hits .... Ernie Banks: 1,009
Batting Average .... Riggs Stevenson: .336
Slugging Average .... Hack Wilson: .590
Consecutive Games .... Billy Wiliams: 1,117
Stolen Bases .... Frank Chance: 404

CAREER PITCHING

Games Won..Charles Root: 201
Games...Charles Root: 605
Years...Charles Root: 16
Shutouts..Mordecai Brown: 48
Strikeouts...Ferguson Jenkins: 1,808
*National League Record
**Tied National League record
†Major League Record

CUBS CAREER SHUTOUT LEADERS— SINCE 1900

Alexander	90	Burdette	33
Brown	55	Tyler	33
Reulbach	42	Derringer	32
French	40	Neff	31
Clarkson	37	Overall	31
Jackson	37	Raffensberger	31
Cooper	36	Warneke	31
Simmons	35	Leifield	30
Vaughn	35	Jenkins	27

CHICAGO CUBS YEAR-BY-YEAR—SINCE 1900

Year	Finish	W-L	PCT	Manager	Attendance
1900	5t	65-75	.464	Loftus	————
1901	5	53-86	.381	Loftus	————
1902	5	68-69	.496	Selee	————
1903	3	82-56	.594	Selee	————
1904	2	93-60	.608	Selee	————
1905	3	92-61	.601	Selee/Chance	————
1906	1	116-36***	.763**	Chance	————
1907	1*	107-45	.704	Chance	————
1908	1*	99-55	.643	Chance	————
1909	2	104-49	.680	Chance	————
1910	1	104-50	.675	Chance	————
1911	2	92-62	.597	Chance	————
1912	3	91-59	.607	Chance	————
1913	3	88-65	.575	Evers	————
1914	4	78-76	.506	O'Day	————
1915	4	73-80	.477	Bresnahan	
1916	5	67-86	.438	Tinker	454,609†
1917	5	74-80	.481	Mitchell	363,748
1918	1	84-45	.651	Mitchell	338,802
1919	3	75-65	.536	Mitchell	421,689
1920	5t	75-79	.487	Mitchell	481,183
1921	7	64-89	.418	Evers/Killefer	410,110
1922	5	80-74	.519	Killefer	541,993
1923	4	83-71	.539	Killefer	705,049
1924	5	81-72	.529	Killefer	720,962
1925	8	68-86	.442	Killefer/Maranville/Gibson	623,030
1926	4	82-72	.532	McCarthy	886,925
1927	4	85-68	.556	McCarthy	1,163,347
1928	3	91-63	.591	McCarthy	1,148,053
1929	1	98-54	.645	McCarthy	1,485,166
1930	2	90-64	.584	McCarthy/Hornsby	1,467,881
1931	3	84-70	.545	Hornsby	1,089,449
1932	1	90-64	.584	Hornsby/Grimm	976,449
1933	3	86-68	.558	Grimm	894,879
1934	3	86-65	.570	Grimm	709,245

Year	Finish	W-L	PCT	Manager	Attendance
1935	1	100-54	.649	Grimm	690,576
1936	2t	87-67	.565	Grimm	701,111
1937	2	93-61	.604	Grimm	897,852
1938	1	89-63	.586	Grimm/Hartnett	955,401
1939	4	84-70	.545	Hartnett	729,309
1940	5	75-79	.487	Hartnett	534,878
1941	6	70-84	.455	Wilson	545,159
1942	6	68-86	.442	Wilson	590,972
1943	5	74-79	.484	Wilson	508,247
1944	4	75-79	.487	Wilson/Grimm	640,110
1945	1	98-56	.636	Grimm	1,036,386
1946	3	82-71	.536	Grimm	1,342,970
1947	6	69-85	.448	Grimm	1,364,039
1948	8	64-90	.416	Grimm	1,237,792
1949	8	61-93	.396	Grimm/Frisch	1,143,139
1950	7	64-89	.418	Frisch	1,165,944
1951	8	62-92	.403	Frisch/Cavarretta	894,415
1952	5	77-77	.500	Cavarretta	1,024,826
1953	7	65-89	.422	Cavarretta	763,653
1954	7	64-90	.416	Hack	748,183
1955	6	72-81	.471	Hack	875,800
1956	8	60-94	.390	Hack	720,118
1957	7t	62-92	.403	Scheffing	670,629
1958	5t	72-82	.468	Scheffing	979,904
1959	5t	74-80	.481	Scheffing	858,255
1960	7	60-94	.390	Grimm/Boudreau	809,770
1961	7	64-90	.416	NONE	673,057
1962	9	59-103	.364	NONE	609,802
1963	7	82-80	.506	NONE	979,551
1964	8	76-86	.496	NONE	751,647
1965	8	72-90	.444	NONE	641,361
1966	10	59,103	.364	Durocher	635,891
1967	3	87-74	.540	Durocher	977,226
1968	3	84-78	.519	Durocher	1,043,409
1969rE	2	92-70	.568	Durocher	1,674,993X
1970	2	84-78	.519	Durocher	1,642,705
1971	3t	83-79	.512	Durocher	1,653,007
1972	2	85-70	.548	Durocher/Lockman	1,229,163
1973	5	77-84	.478	Lockman	1,351,705
1974	6	66-96	.407	Lockman/Marshall	1,015,378
1975	5t	75-87	.463	Marshall	1,034,819
1976	4	75-87	.463	Marshall	1,026,217
1977	4	81-81	.500	Franks	1,439,834
1978	3	79-83	.488	Franks	1,525,311
1979	5	80-82	.494	Franks/Amalfitano	1,648,587
1980	6	64-98	.395	Gomez/Amalfitano	1,192,070

*World Champions
**Highest won-loss percentage/major league record
***Most Wins, one season/major leagues
XHighest season attended for Cubs
†First year in Wrigley Field

t: tie
E: Eastern Division play began

INDEX

INDEX

Page numbers in *italics* indicate photographs.